Louis R. Ehrich

The Question of Silver

Comprising a Summary of Legislation in the United States

Louis R. Ehrich

The Question of Silver
Comprising a Summary of Legislation in the United States

ISBN/EAN: 9783744730419

Printed in Europe, USA, Canada, Australia, Japan

Cover: Foto ©Suzi / pixelio.de

More available books at **www.hansebooks.com**

COMPRISING A BRIEF SUMMARY OF LEGISLATION IN THE UNITED
STATES, TOGETHER WITH A PRACTICAL ANALYSIS OF THE
PRESENT SITUATION, AND OF THE ARGUMENTS
OF THE ADVOCATES OF UNLIMITED
SILVER COINAGE

BY

LOUIS R. EHRICH

OF COLORADO

G. P. PUTNAM'S SONS

NEW YORK   LONDON
27 WEST TWENTY-THIRD STREET   24 BEDFORD STREET, STRAND

The Knickerbocker Press

1892

Electrotyped, Printed, and Bound by
The Knickerbocker Press, New York
G. P. Putnam's Sons

TO THE READER.

THE first of the following Papers, in response to a special invitation, was read before "The Monday Evening Club,"—a literary society composed of gentlemen connected with The First Congregational Church of this city, —on December 8th, 1891. Thirty-five gentlemen were present. After the reading of the Paper, a motion condemning the "Free and unlimited coinage of Silver" was carried unanimously; followed by a motion requesting the publication of the Paper. It was accordingly published in the *Colorado Springs Gazette* of December 13th, 1891.

The second Paper, which is a "Reply to a reply," offers its own explanation of its originating cause.

That, in this year of grace 1892, a movement like "Free and unlimited Silver coinage," regardless of international co-operation, is believed to command a majority in both Houses of Congress, shows what the inertia of the thinking conservative fraction of the American people can, and may yet, lead to. There should be no delay in distributing, as widely as possible, whatever literature will educate the public as to the character, the principles, and the history of Money.

Louis R. Ehrich.

Colorado Springs, Colorado,
Jan 28th, 1892.

THE QUESTION OF SILVER.

The history of civilization has a gold and silver lining. From early antiquity, man has recognized that the best instruments for mediums of exchange and for measures of value are gold and silver. As tersely expressed by an eminent geologist: "Indestructible, uncreatable, readily divisible, easily coined, widely distributed, but nowhere abundant, they have been proved by long experience unique in their adaptation to the wants of society as representatives of value and as circulating media."

It would be a fascinating study to trace the influence of the precious metals upon civilization and to show how the rise and fall in the production of gold and silver has variously affected the well-being of man. For this, time is lacking, and we shall be compelled to confine our attention to the movements and influences of gold and silver in the Nine teenth century, giving more particular study to the financial history of our own country.

The Constitution of the United States, framed in 1787, contains the following provisions: Congress shall have power "to coin money, regulate the value thereof, and of foreign coin, and fix the standard of weights and measures." (Sec. 8, Art. I). "No state shall coin money; emit bills of credit; make anything but gold and silver coin a tender in payment of debts." (Sec. 10, Art. I.)

Five years before, Robert Morris and Thomas Jefferson had agitated the establishment of an American mint. It is interesting that Morris, who was "the superintendent of finance," was a monometallist. He advocated the use of silver alone, because, as he said, gold and silver could not be used as a standard on account of the variation in the ratio of the two metals. The subject was discussed for several years until, in 1791, Alexander Hamilton brought in his "report on the establishment of a mint." Differing from Morris, he emphatically argued, that if a single standard were to be adopted, owing to its greater stability, the metal should be gold; but that, for fear of abridging the quantity of the circulating medium, he favored the double standard. The question was as to the ratio to be established between gold and silver.

There was a difference of opinion on this subject, but Hamilton concluded that the commercial ratio, based on American values, was 1 to 15; that is, that an ounce of gold was worth fifteen times as much as an ounce of silver. The recommendations of Hamilton were accepted by Congress with slight modifications. The Act of 1792 declared that the gold dollar should consist of 24.75 grains of pure gold, that the silver dollar should consist of fifteen times as many grains, namely 371.25 grains of pure silver, that there should be free and unlimited coinage of either metal, and that either gold or silver coins, as issued from the United States mint, should be a legal tender. In Washington's sixth annual address, issued 1794, I find the following allusion:

"The mint of the United States has entered upon the coinage of the precious metals, and considerable sums of defective coins and bullion have been lodged with the director by individuals. There is a pleasing prospect that the institution will, at no remote day, realize the expectation which was originally formed of its utility."

Our most reliable experts agree that in the year 1793 the commercial ratio of gold to silver was just about 1:15. But from that very year silver, relatively to gold, began to cheapen. In 1795 it was about 15½:1. In 1799, about 15¾:1. For the forty years from 1793 to 1833 it oscillated up and down, but it never again rose to the ratio of 15.1. The country was sparsely populated, intercommunication was slow and irregular, there were neither railroads nor steam-ships—the demand for metallic money was very great—and yet before long, there came into operation the effect of the simple law known as Gresham's law, named after Sir Thomas Gresham, a very successful London merchant who founded "The Royal Exchange" the year after Shakespeare was born. Gresham's law is that "bad money drives out good money." This law is as simple and as inevitable as the fact that if ninety-nine cents will pay debts just as well as 100 cents, people will, as soon as they have discovered the fact, pay only the ninety-nine cents; or, if merchants find that fifteen ounces will satisfy their customers for a pound avoirdupois just as well as sixteen ounces, they will naturally, if the law justifies and protects them, deal out only the fifteen ounces. Gresham's law may also be stated thus: If two metals are legal tender, are coined at a fixed ratio and both are entitled to free coinage, if there is any variation in value, only the cheaper metal will circulate.

Early in the century, Gresham's law began

to exert its influence on the American coined metals. On the average gold was worth 3 per cent. more, as to silver, than the value stamped on the gold coin. Gold began to disappear certainly as early as 1810. It has occurred to me whether the fact that no silver dollars were coined after 1805 did not result from the observation of the gradual disappearance of gold and the hope that by making silver dollars more scarce their value might relatively rise. At all events, the fact stands that about 1819 the circulation of gold coin was almost completely extinguished in the United States. In 1814 the gold coinage of the United States mint was $77,000. In 1815 it was $3,000. In 1816 it was *nil*.

Various suggestions were made in Congress. In 1831 Mr. Campbell P. White made the following sound statement:

"There are inherent and incurable defects in the system which regulates the standard of value in both gold and silver; its instability as a measure of contracts and mutability as the practical currency of a nation, are serious imperfections: whilst impossibility of maintaining both metals in concurrent, simultaneous or promiscuous circulation, appears to be clearly ascertained."

In a report made the following year he writes:

"The committee cannot ascertain that both metals have ever circulated simultaneously, concurrently and indiscriminately in any country where there are banks or money dealers; and they entertain the conviction that the nearest approach to an invariable standard is its establishment in one metal, which metal shall compose exclusively the currency for large payments."

The first experiment of the United States with the free and unlimited coinage of gold and silver closed in 1834. In that year, what is known as the Act of 1834, changing the ratio, was enacted. In a speech, delivered on the floor of the Senate in 1834, Thomas H. Benton said:

"The false valuation put upon gold has rendered the mint of the United States, so far as the gold coinage is concerned, a most ridiculous and absurd institution. It has coined, and that at a large expense to the United States, 2,262,177 pieces of gold, worth $11,852,890, and where are the pieces now? Not one of them to be seen! all sold, and exported! and so regular is the operation that the director of the mint, in his latest report to Congress, says that the new-coined gold frequently remains in the mint, uncalled for, though ready for delivery, until the day arrives for a packet to sail to Europe. He calculates that two millions of native gold will be coined annually hereafter; the whole of which, without a reform of the gold standard, will be conducted, like exiles, from the national mint to the seashore, and transported to foreign regions."

In another part of the same speech, he says that he must bring out certain facts.

"To enable the friends of GOLD to go to work at the right place to effect the recovery of that precious metal WHICH THEIR FATHERS ONCE POSSESSED—which the subjects of European kings now possess—which the citizens of the young republics to the south all possess—which even the free negroes of San Domingo possess—but which the yeomanry of this America have been deprived of for more than twenty years, and will be deprived of for ever, unless they discover the cause of the evil, and apply the remedy to its root."

It is rather amusing in the face of the present cry for "the silver dollar of the daddies," to listen to this cry of the men of 1834 for the gold dollar of their daddies.

The coinage act of June 1834 fixed the legal ratio of gold to silver as 1:16. The commercial ratio was nearly 1:15.3-5. By the Act of 1792, silver was over-valued. By the Act of 1834, gold was over-valued. The framers of the Act of 1792 thought that they were bimetallists, but they were, in fact, silver monometallists. The framers of the Act of 1834 thought that they were bimetallists, but they were, in fact, gold monometallists.

Some members of Congress saw the danger. A Mr. Gorham, of Massachusetts, said:

"I warn the house not to bring about, by hasty legislation, the same state of things in relation to silver which has heretofore existed respecting gold. . . . If the law makes gold too cheap, the country will have no silver circulation. We shall soon have the same cry about the want of silver coin which there was now about gold."

In the sixteen years after 1834, the commercial ratio of silver to gold oscillated from 15 3-4:1 to 15 9-10:1, but it never fell to the ratio of 16:1. Consequently, the silver as coined by the United States was, relatively to gold, worth more than its coin value. Gresham's law again came into play and silver disappeared from circulation. The silver dollar was rarely used as money after 1840. Professor Simon Newcomb wrote in 1879 :

"It would probably be safe to assert that. . . . one-half of the citizens of our country, born since 1840, had never seen a United States silver dollar."

In the period from 1841 to 1851, ten years, the annual average of the total world's production of gold was, in round figures, $38,000,000; of silver $34,000,000. As you observe, a production not very unequal. In 1849 and 1851 came the remarkable gold discoveries of California, Australia and Russia. In the five years from 1851 to 1855, the average total world's production of silver was, in round figures, $40,000,000, of gold $140,000,000. This inequality of production gave a still higher value to silver, and whereas the commercial ratio of silver to gold was 15¾:1 in 1834, it rose to 15⅓:1 in 1853.

In the coinage act of 1792 a serious error had been committed, which was re-enacted in the Act of 1837 supplementary to the coinage act of 1834; namely, the subsidiary coins, the half-dollars, quarter-dollars, dimes and half-dimes, had been minted with their exact proportion of the silver contained in the dollar. Consequently, after 1834, and more especially after the vast increase of gold-production, Gresham's law operated not only as regards the silver dollar, but also as regards the smaller coins as well. In 1853, Dr. C. L. Dunham said in Congress:

"There is, then, a constant stimulant to gather up every silver coin, and send it to market as bullion to be exchanged for gold, and the result is the country is almost devoid of small change for the ordinary small business transactions, and what we have is of a depreciated character."

The coinage act of 1853 remedied the error of 1792. Instead of leaving in the half-dollar the exact half of the standard silver contained in the dollar—namely, 206¼ grains —this act cut down the standard silver of the half-dollar to 192 grains, with the smaller coins in proportion. No free coinage of these subsidiary coins was allowed. Their legal tender value was limited to five dollars. Thus the Act of 1853 reduced the silver of the fractional coins about 7 per cent.—and as the silver dollar was only worth about 3½ per cent. more than the gold dollar, all profit in melting the subsidiary coins ceased.

Now this coinage act of 1853 is remarkable in its *omissions*. Mind you, the silver dollar had practically gone out of circulation. The total coinage of silver dollars in 1850 had been $47,500; in 1851, $1,300; in 1852, $1,100. In contrast, the total gold coinage of 1852 was over $56,000,000, of which $2,000,000 was in gold dollars. Why was there no shriek then for "the dollar of the daddies"? Simply because there was nobody financially interested in shrieking. For the five years 1851 to 1855, the average silver production of the United States was, in round figures, $375,000; the average gold production, $62,000,000. The truth is, that the committee which drafted the bill, and Congress itself, virtually understood and believed that the coinage of the United States in 1853 was settled on a gold standard. Mr. Dunham, one of the finance committee, in replying to another plan proposed, said on the floor of the

House : " We should thereby still continue the double standard of gold and silver, a thing the committee desire to obviate. They desire to have the standard currency consist of gold only."

From 1853 to 1862 it did consist of gold only. The silver dollar was during those years worth an average of $3\frac{1}{2}$ cents above the dollar stamp, and none were in circulation.

On the morning of April 13, 1861, the *New York Herald* contained the following despatch, dated Charleston, April 12 :

"The first shot at Fort Sumter from Stevens' battery was fired by the venerable Edmund Ruffin of Virginia."

We were soon in the throes of the rebellion. The government needed money. In the fall of '61 it borrowed $100,000,000 in gold from the banks. In 1862 the issue of unsecured legal tender paper money was agitated in Congress. Gold at once sprang to a premium. The legal tender bill passed Congress in February, 1862. One hundred and fifty millions of what we afterwards called "greenbacks" were issued at once. Gresham's law began to operate immediately. Gold disappeared from circulation. The average gold premium of February was $3\frac{1}{2}$ per cent., of March $1\frac{3}{4}$ per cent., of April $1\frac{7}{8}$

per cent., of May 3⅛ per cent. When the 150,000,000 had been issued in February it had been stated that that sum would probably be the maximum issue. In July, however, another issue of 150,000,000 was made. The average premium of gold in July rose to 14½ per cent. Gresham's law put on additional steam and our silver half-dollars, quarters, dimes and half-dimes were also driven out of circulation. The odious "shin-plasters" were decreed July 17, 1862. Gold advanced to a premium of 24 per cent. in September, 34 per cent. in December, 60 per cent. in January, 1863, and then went up and down until it reached its highest point of 185 per cent. in July, 1864. The resumption of silver subsidiary payments in 1877 and of gold payments in 1879 we need not dwell on.

We return now to the extraordinary production of gold after 1850. In the twenty years from 1830 to 1850, the total world's production of gold was about $525,000,000. In the twenty years from 1850 to 1870, the total world's production was about $2,725,000,000, more than five times as much. It has been computed that the gold product from 1851 to 1875 exceeded the entire gold product for the 357 years preceding, namely, from the year of the discovery of America to 1850. This vast increase in gold production created some alarm. It was feared that it might seriously disarrange values. The purchasing power of gold fell and commodities rose considerably in value. Some French economists even discussed the possible demonetization of gold. However, the leading economists of the great nations of the world soon realized that this was a favorable opportunity to place the business of the world on a gold basis. Gold was recognized as the best instrument for this purpose. The International Monetary Conference held at Paris in 1867, laid down as a leading principle necessary to universal coinage "the universal adoption of a single gold standard."

The great war indemnity which France was compelled to pay Germany after her defeat in 1870-71 was paid in gold. Germany, following the advice of her best financial heads, hurried to place herself on the single gold standard, which was effected by the Acts of 1871 and 1873.

We now come to what is called "the conspiracy against silver"—the demonetization of silver in the United States in 1873. The charge was first made in 1876, and we hear now again and again that the silver dollar was "demonetized by a trick," that hardly anybody knew anything about at the time—that "silver was struck down in the night," etc., etc. What are the undeniable facts? As far back as April 25, 1870, the Hon. Geo. S. Boutwell, then secretary of the treasury, transmitted to the Senate of the United States the draft of a bill now known as the coinage act of Feb. 12, 1873. This bill was a revision of all laws relating to the mint coinage. *It omitted the silver dollar-piece.* The Senate took no immediate action, but sent copies of the bill to some thirty experts on coinage matters in the United States for an expression of their opinion.* In their replies, Mr. Elliott says: "The bill proposes the discontinuance of the silver dollar." Mr. Patterson says: "By this amendment, gold becomes the standard of money, of which the gold dollar is the unit. Silver is subsidiary." Mr. Snowden writes: "I see that it is proposed to demonetize the silver dollar." The House of Representatives called for these expert replies, and they were accordingly forwarded by the Senate. As early as Jan. 10, 1871, the bill passed in the Senate by a vote of 36 to 14. The bill was then sent to and fro for several years. That its character

---

*The above statement was based on Document No. 1453, Treasury Department, entitled "A Brief History of Coinage Legislation in the United States." I am glad to make a correction by stating that it was the Hon. John Jay Knox who sent out the bill for expert opinion. The reader is referred to the highly interesting and most instructive "Interview of John Jay Knox before 'The committee on Coinage, Weights and Measures,' Saturday February 21, 1891,"—issued from the Government Printing-office.

was perfectly understood and perfectly explained is shown by the following quotations of speeches delivered in the House. Mr. Kelley of Pennsylvania said:

"I again call attention of the House to the fact that the gentlemen who oppose this bill insist upon maintaining a silver dollar worth 3½ cents more than the gold dollar, and that so long as these provisions remain you cannot keep silver coin in the country."

Mr. Stoughton of Michigan said:

"Gold is practically the standard of value among all civilized nations and the time has come in this country when the gold dollar shall be distinctly declared to be the coin representative of the money unit."

The bill was printed *thirteen times* by order of Congress. It was discussed during five different sessions. The debates on the bill in the Congressional Globe occupy 148 *pages*, and yet serious men have the effrontery to tell us that the contents of the bill were not known. On Jan. 14, 1891, Mr. Ingalls, a rabid free coinage man, referring to the coinage bill of 1873, made the following statement on the floor of the Senate:

"That bill was pending in its various stages for four years in both Houses of Congress. It passed both Houses by decided majorities. It was read and re-read and reprinted thirteen times, as appears by the records. It was commented on in the newspapers; it was the subject of discussion in financial bodies all over the country, and yet we have the concurrent testimony of every senator and every member of the House of Representatives who was present during the time that the legislation was pending and proceeding that he knew nothing whatever about the demonetization of silver and the destruction of the coinage of the silver dollar. The senator from Nevada (Mr. Stewart) who knows so many things, felt called upon to make a speech of an hour's duration to show that he knew nothing whatever about it. I have heard others declaim and with one consent make excuse that they knew nothing about it. It is one of the phenomena and anomalies of legislation and I have no other explanation to make than this: I believe that both Houses of Congress and the President of the United States must have been HYPNOTIZED."

"What is the true explanation? The fact is that in 1873 silver had demonetized itself. The coin in the silver dollar was still worth a little more than a dollar, and it has been estimated that there were not, at that time, a thousand standard silver dollars in existence. All had been melted or exported. For twenty-eight years the ounce price of silver had not fallen below $1.30, whereas its coinage ratio to gold was $1.29; and in 1873 it still stood within one-fifth of one cent of $1.30. The silver producers were indifferent as to the law of 1873 because, unbrokenly for forty years, silver had been worth more than its coinage value.

Beginning with 1870, the gold product began to decline, the silver product began to increase enormously. In 1874, the Latin-Union, noticing the downward tendency of silver, withdrew the privilege of free coinage and limited the coinage of the silver five-franc pieces to a moderate amount. Silver in 1874 fell to $1.27 an ounce. In '75 to $1.24 an ounce. In '76 to $1.15 an ounce. *Then and not till then*, began to be heard the cry of "the conspiracy of 1873."

Silver has been struck down, but not by the bill of 1873, nor by any bill concocted by man. The hand which struck down silver is the hand which will strike us all down in time, the hand which nothing can withstand, *the irresistible hand of Nature*. Silver has been struck down by one of the natural forces, by the great law of demand and supply. The yearly average of gold production in the twenty-five years from 1851-75 was $127,000,-000. The yearly average product of silver for the same period was $51,000,000. The average annual product of gold for the fifteen years from 1876 to 1890 *declined* to $108,000,-000; a minus of 15 per cent. The average annual product of silver for the same period *increased* to $116,000,000; a plus of 127 per cent. *There is the whole silver question*, and in face of these facts, it is as now impossible for the United States, single-handed, with free and unlimited coinage, to bring silver to a parity with gold on any such basis as 16:1, *it is more impossible* than for a thousand men to pick up our great "Pike's Peak" and transport it bodily to Denver.

In 1876, as before stated, silver had fallen to $1.15 an ounce. Free silver coinage bills were introduced in the House of Representatives by Mr. Kelley and Mr. Bland. In the fall of 1877 a free coinage bill passed the House. In the Senate the free coinage feature was cut out and the bill, as amended by Mr. Allison, passed February, 1878. The House, accepting the Senate amendments, passed the bill. President Hayes vetoed it, but it was passed over his veto. The bill of 1878, generally spoken of as the "Bland" bill, directed the secretary of the treasury to purchase not less than two million nor more than four million dollars' worth of silver bullion per month, to coin it into silver dollars, said silver dollars to be full legal tender at "their nominal value." Also, that the holder of ten or more of these silver dollars could exchange them for silver certificates, said certificates being "receivable for customs, taxes and all public dues." The bill was pushed and passed by the efforts, principally, of the greenback inflationists and the representatives of the silver States. If the Bland-Allison bill had not made the coinage of silver obligatory, I could make no objection to it. Since 1878, 405,000,000 silver dollars have been coined. Of these 348,000,000 are still lying in the treasury vaults. No comment is needed. The Bland-Allison act did not hold up silver. In 1879 it was worth $1.12 an ounce, in 1880 $1.14, '81 $1.13, '82 $1.13, '83 $1.11, '86 99 cents, until in '89 it reached 93½ cents an ounce. That is, in 1889 the commercial ratio was 22:1 and the coin value of the Bland-Allison silver dollar was 72 cents.

In March, 1890, a bill was reported to the House by the committee of "coinage, weights and measures," based on a plan proposed by Secretary Windom, to the effect: That any owner of silver bullion, not foreign, could bring it to any mint, and obtain legal tender treasury notes therefor equal to the market value of the silver, redeemable, on demand, either in gold or in silver bullion (at its then value) at the government's option, or in silver dollars at the holder's option. The bill passed the House. The Senate passed it with an amendment making provision for free and unlimited coinage. It finally went to a conference committee which reported the bill that became a law, July 14, 1890. This bill directs the secretary of the treasury to purchase four and one-half million ounces of silver a month at the market price, to give legal tender treasury notes therefor, said notes being redeemable in gold or silver coin at the option of the government, "it being the established policy of the United States to maintain the two metals on a parity with each other upon the present legal ratio." It was believed that this bill would raise the price of silver. So all the silver men confidently prophesied. In January '90—silver was worth 97½ cents an ounce. In March 96 cents. Anticipating favorable silver legislation, silver speculators drove silver to $1.00½; in April, to $1.05; in May, to $1.08; in August to $1.15, and finally to $1.21 on September 3d. Speculators, however, count for little against natural law. The price began to decline to $1.09 in October, to $1.06 in December, and its price, with slight fluctuations, has been steadily downward ever since. Remember that the price of an ounce of silver averaged 97½ cents in January, 1890. This morning's (Dec. 8, 1891.) quotation for an ounce of silver was 94½ cents an ounce. To-day the silver in our dollar is actually worth 73 cents. The silver men are disappointed. Their bill of 1890 brought a customer into the market who purchased fifty-four million ounces a year, and yet silver is lower than when that bill passed. They cannot realize that it is impossible to fight against a natural law.

The cry grows louder and louder for free and unlimited silver coinage. In the din of the battle, two very distinct rallying cries can be distinguished. One is the desire to get $1.29 instead of 95 cents for an ounce of silver. The other is, the desire to assist the debtor class to lighten the burden of indebtedness. Strangely enough, these cries are generally emitted by the same silver enthusiasts, and still more strangely they are diametrically opposed to each. If free and unlimited silver coinage will make the silver dollar fully equal in value to the gold dollar, then the silver dollar will be just as hard to get as the gold dollar, and the debtor will be disappointed by standing just where he stands to-day. If, on the other hand, free coinage does not increase the value of silver and the silver dollar as now will intrinsically be worth seventy-three cents, then the debtor will make a large saving in his debt payment and the silver-mine owner will be disappointed just in that proportion.

Let us now see whether free silver coinage

will play into the hands of the debtor or of the silver-mine owner. \The first effect of the free and unlimited coinage of silver would be the immediate and total disappearance of gold from circulation. The ink of the President's signature to the bill would not be dry before gold would be at a premium. Why? If you had any article which you had reason to believe would jump 25 to 33 per cent. in price within a few days or a few weeks, what would you do with it? You would hold on to it. The day after the enactment of the free coinage bill you could exchange your gold for silver at the market price, have it coined into dollars and make the difference. But you reply: "No American would sell it to you." Certainly not—but Mexico is handy, and there is a stock of $3,800,000,000 of silver in the world to draw from. Silver would, at first, advance without a doubt; but it would have to advance fully to $1.29 an ounce and to remain at that value not to permanently drive out gold. If it reached even $1.28, gold would still be driven from circulation.

"But"—say the silver-men, "*it will reach and remain at $1.29 an ounce.*" This, in face of the fact, that there is no demand for silver in Europe, that the European nations most friendly to silver have suspended its coinage some twelve years—that the supply of silver is increasing, and that any rise in value would stimulate its production enormously. Is nothing to be learned from history? When the United States established the ratio of 16:1 in 1834,—a gold dollar, 23.2 grains of pure gold, was worth a fraction less than 99 cents as compared with silver. Gold had free and unlimited coinage all over the world. All the nations had a large and increasing demand for it, and yet it took just forty years to make 23.2 grains of pure gold equal to 371¼ grains of pure silver, that is, to make a gold dollar equal in value to a silver dollar, in spite of the fact that in those forty years, the United States coined 878,000,000 dollars of gold. Why? Because the law of supply and demand held it down. Remember, please, that the difference was only a fraction over one cent, and yet silver enthusiasts really believe and want sane men to believe that against the inexorable law of supply and demand, the magic of free coinage is quickly going to wipe out the present difference of 27 cents between the silver and the gold dollar. *It is impossible.*

Free coinage must be followed by the immediate disappearance of gold. This will, to some extent, mean contraction, but not to the extent that many suppose. Far worse in its baneful effect than the gold disappearance will be the immediate and far-reaching shock to confidence, the unwillingness to embark in new enterprises, to extend business, to loan money, or to take any business risks. Such a shock means panic and resulting ruin to thousands. The whole country will suffer, but the States which will suffer the most are the Western States, the very States which are trying to bring about free silver coinage, the States which most especially are dependent for their development on the investment of outside capital. The value of the silver dollar will oscillate up and down with the oscillation of the price of the silver ounce; and until these oscillations become comparatively small, no prudent man will want to engage in a business venture. This oscillation of silver will be a constant obstacle in business. It will be like doing business with a yardstick or a quart measure which grows smaller or bigger every day. Silver-men declare against having silver a commodity like wheat, cotton or pork. Well, with free silver coinage, silver would not be a commodity in the United States. That is, the bullion value and the coinage value would be exactly the same thing in purchasing power. But would it not be a commodity just the same in Europe? Would we not, just the same, get a daily report of the ounce or commodity price of silver in London? And would not the rise and fall of this ounce price have to be taken into account by every shrewd man of business?

Now, where will silver stand when the oscillations become small? I venture to predict that it will stand *even below the present silver price. The debtor classes will have won the day.*

When a Western man speaks of the debtor classes he generally means the Western farmers. The free silver coinage advocate proposes to put a depreciated silver dollar in the hands of the farmer so that he can confiscate twenty-five per cent. of the money his creditor loaned him. Most silver-men would shrink with loathing from a proposition to allow the farmer to make every fourth dollar he paid his creditor a counterfeit, and yet that will be the *practical* effect of unlimited coinage. If the Kansas and Nebraska farmers are to be an object of charity, I would vastly prefer to have the government of the United States pay twenty-five per cent. of their indebtedness rather than have the public views of honesty debauched by enabling a debtor to cheat his creditor. But says some objector: "Money is worth more now than when the farmer borrowed." Let us see. Most silver advocates claim that the more money there is in the country, the better for the farmer, the easier for him to pay his debts. Hardly a farm mortgage of the West runs for more than five years, so nearly all the mortgages due in 1891 were made in 1886; and yet, there are two hundred and fifty millions more money in the country now than there was in '86.

We hear much as to these debtor classes. Suppose we enquire as to who their creditor is. Many people think that the money borrowed by the Western farmer has come from the rich Eastern, "gold bug." What are the facts? The vast majority of Western farm mortgages are below a thousand dollars in value, and they are held almost exclusively by people of very moderate means in the New England States. Old people who have passed the age of accumulation and who, by a life of economy, have amassed a small competency, widows and unmarried women who must live on a fixed income, small tradesmen who, by thrift and earnest work, have put by a few thousand dollars—these are the classes whom it is proposed to despoil in the name of law. Woe to the Western farmer if he attempts it! The day of retribution will come when his necessities will drive him to ask for another loan. The truth is that the Western farmer has not paid exorbitant interest. I feel confident that the facts will bear out my statement, that the Kansas and Nebraska farmer to-day pays a lower rate of interest than the Denver merchant for his business loans.

No! The creditor of the Western farmers is not the Eastern "gold bug." Rich men are not lenders of money. They are borrowers the world over. Your bankers will tell you that the great majority of their deposit accounts are small accounts. The safety of banks, their ability to loan money freely, lies in those small accounts. Most of the money loaned by banks is loaned to rich men. They are borrowers because they know what to do with the money. It pays them to borrow. Take the great buildings owned by the rich men of Denver. All carry mortgages. From whom has the money come? From the savings banks, from the insurance companies—in other words, from the combined savings of the people of moderate means.

Yet the greatest creditor class and the one which will suffer most from free and unlimited silver coinage is the labor class—the miner, the servant, the mechanic. Every man who works for wages is a creditor in the evening, at the end of the week, or at the end of the month. He will be the last to discover how a depreciated dollar defrauds him and that he is daily meeting a loss by its decreased purchasing power. The miner will take his $3.50 a day long after it must be exchanged for commodities which formerly cost him a dollar less. Andrew Jackson says most truly in his eighth annual message :

"A depreciation of the currency is always attended by a loss to the laboring classes. This portion of the community have neither time nor opportunity to watch the ebbs and flows of the money market. Engaged from day to day in their useful toils, they do not perceive that, although their wages are nominally the same, or even somewhat higher, they are greatly reduced in fact by the rapid increase of currency which, as it appears to make money abound, they are at first inclined to consider a blessing."

Evidently this question of free silver coinage is more than a question of finance—it is a question of morals—it is a question of philanthropy.

Prices must naturally rise to compare with the value of silver. In process of time, the wage-worker will understand his position and will demand and obtain higher wages in proportion. During the interval, however, which will be long, he will be literally defrauded.

There is another feature of debt-payment which deserves consideration. If it will be cheaper and easier to pay debts in silver which, by the terms of contract, can be paid in silver, it will be correspondingly more difficult and more expensive to pay debts which are made payable in gold. Leaving aside the vast railroad bond indebtedness, all of which is payable in gold, and all of which eventually must be paid by the whole people, let us look nearer home. All the bonds of private corporations—like water works, street railroads, etc.,—all the county and municipal bonds are payable in gold, principal and interest. There is not a city or county in Colorado which will not suffer financial hardship, there is not a Colorado property-owner who will not be forced to pay increased taxes in order to enable the Kansas and Nebraska farmer to "fleece" his Eastern creditor.

But we hear a silver man who says: "These are all theories. You cannot prove by practical national experience that these theories are correct." Let us look about. Here is Mexico right under our nose! When the United States and all the European nations demonetized silver in the seventies—Mexico kept right on. It gave free and unlimited coinage to both gold and silver. What was then the inevitable consequence? Twenty years ago, gold and silver circulated in Mexico. To-day, not a gold coin circulates there. The Mexican silver dollar circulates alone and is worth just the silver that is in it. Prices have adjusted themselves to it. The Mexican dollar, containing six more grains of pure silver than the American dollar, is worth about seventy-five cents, and when a Mexican exchanges his dollar for American money he gets *even less than the bullion value of the silver in his dollar*. Mexico is a very near at hand illustration of the operation of Gresham's law.

" But, " argues some persistent free silver man—" let us grant all the results you claim : The disappearance of gold, the first shock to business, the injustice to the creditor—the wrong to the wageworker, the increased difficulty of gold payments, etc., etc. Yet after the worst has been suffered, after everything has found its equilibrium in silver—prices, wages, etc.,—shall we not then be in good financial and business shape?" The reply is clear. We certainly would be, if we only exchanged commodities among ourselves, if we could profitably consume in the United States all that we produce. But we cannot. Our production is far beyond our power of consumption—and our only salvation is to go out into the markets of the world and sell our surplus. There is where a silver basis will do us constant and incalculable injury, and the man who will be most seriously and most constantly injured will be the American farmer.

The American farmer has had many drawbacks, but one blessing he has hitherto enjoyed. There might be speculation in his product, but there could be no speculation in the money with which his product was paid. He sold on a gold basis. With a silver basis, the exporter who bought his wheat or his corn, for a foreign order, would have to calculate or speculate on a possible decline in silver between the date of his foreign exchange draft and the date of its payment. The exporter would, necessarily, be compelled to calculate on the risk and to deduct a percentage from the purchasing price he would otherwise pay. Who would lose this percentage? The American farmer. Within a period of six years the farmer would lose far more through this channel than any mistaken profit by a 25 per cent. debt repudiation.

The same loss would come in the export of every American product. In the great international race for business, we should be like the runner who would enter a foot race wearing heavy high-topped boots. We should be handicapped. International trade-preference is a question of very small percentages. As Daniel Webster said in 1815:

"The circulating medium of a commercial community must be that which is also the circulating medium of other commercial communities, or must be capable of being converted into that medium without loss. It must be able, not only to pass in payments and receipts among individuals of the same society and nation, but to adjust and discharge the balance of exchanges between different nations."

One final question, the silver man might ask: "Would you favor free silver coinage under any possible condition?" Answer: Yes. Don't make it a legal tender—that means, don't force any one to take it who doesn't want it, and there is no financial objection to the free and unlimited coinage of silver.

How about free coinage of the American silver product only? I can see some basis of reason in this proposition. I can clearly see that that, at least, is going to benefit somebody. The free coinage of the world's silver product would, in my opinion, on the five year basis—not benefit a single class. The greatest eventual sufferer would be the silver-mine owner. But, with the free coinage restricted to the American product, the silver-mine owner would undoubtedly, until gold went to a premium, make the difference between the market value and the coin value of silver—to-day about thirty-four cents an ounce. In others words, the people of the United States would pay the owners of American silver-mines an annual bounty of about eighteen millions of dollars. Silver would be protected to that amount. Waiving the question of protection, certainly there is as good an argument for protecting the silver of the West as for protecting the iron and steel of the East. Assuredly, it would be much cheaper for the people of the United States to make a gift to the silver-mine owners of eighteen millions a year than to suffer the hundred-fold greater loss incident to free and unlimited silver coinage. Couple a law allowing free coinage of the American product with a proviso providing for cessation of silver coinage, whenever gold appreciated to a premium and until the equilibrium had been restored for a certain period, and I should be perfectly satisfied. Colorado would then be getting about nine millions a year more for its silver product than at present—and it would be an object-lesson in protection which might be worth the expense.

One consideration which puzzled me for a long time was, as to how so many intelligent and undoubtedly sincere men could defend unlimited silver coinage. The explanation finally dawned upon me. The resolution passed by "The Trans-mississippi Congress, May 22, 1891, reads: "Resolved, That we are in favor of bimetallism." The Mining Congress of Denver, Nov. 21, adopted the resolution: "Resolved, That the first National Mining Congress is unalterably in favor of the principles of bimetallism." The fact is that the free coinage silver men, instead of understanding that they are silver monometallists, really believe that they are bimetallists, and they are deceived by the many strong and sound arguments of bimetallism into believing that these arguments uphold free and unlimited coinage.

I have no time, at present, to present at length the very interesting monometallic and bimetallic arguments. Briefly told, the monometallist believes that the world's demonetization of silver is a good thing, that the improvements in the methods of facilitating exchanges makes a very large stock of coin unnecessary, that prices have fallen since 1875 not because the value of gold has appreciated, but because the facilities of transportation and improved machinery have made production exceed the world's demand. The bimetallist believes that the demonetization of silver did unnecessarily add to the purchasing power of gold, that it added to the burden of long deferred gold-debt payments, that the business of the world would be safer if founded on the broader base of both metals, and that consequently silver ought to be reinstated throughout Europe and the United States as a money metal.

I am a bimetallist. I understand that as against the vast sum of world exchanges, the addition of silver to the coin of Europe and America would be only a drop in the bucket. But when business strain comes, when the lack of confidence demands actual coin payment, then I want the benefit of even that single drop.

I am in favor of coining all American silver until the limit of a gold premium is reached. When gold goes to a premium, I want silver coinage to stop. The secretary of the treasury should be clothed with power to stop it. None of the free-coinage men can object to this. The Trans-mississippi Congress said:

"Resolved, That we are in favor of all such legislation as will restore the parity of value between gold and silver."

The National Mining Congress said:

"Resolved, That gold and silver, not one to the exclusion of the other, are the money metals of the Constitution."

The fact is that such a proviso would

help powerfully to prevent a premium in gold.

What position should thinking, conservative men take in this matter? Some men say to me : "Let these extremists shout themselves hoarse. They will accomplish nothing." Others say: "We have faith in the good sense of the American people. They will not jump into so dangerous an experiment."

In the first place, I claim, that duty demands outspokenness in this matter.

The people of Colorado are led to believe that we are a unit on this question. They think that not only their political leaders but that their bankers and strong financial and business men are all unanimous for unlimited silver coinage. They should be undeceived. They should as far as possible, have the question explained to them. But aside from this, I maintain that the whole country is suffering from this unceasing silver agitation. With the late European experience that the safest investments are American securities—with our most bountiful harvest at a period when demand is producing high prices—the United States ought to be in a period of most unusual prosperity. But it is not. Why? Because of this silver agitation. Even the silver extremists admit this. Senator Vest of Missouri said in the Senate last January :

"Nothing is so timid as capital, and to-day this silver question is throwing its pall over all the industries and interests of the people of the United States because of the uncertainty which attends it."

The whole country suffers from it, but Colorado most especially. Development in this State is temporarily paralyzed. No money comes here for investment. Business is dull. Land attracts no purchasers. We are being injured more every month than a 33 per cent. bounty on Colorado silver would benefit us in a year. We are dragging the name of Colorado in the dust. We are besmirching the reputation of the State. Colorado is being branded in the East as the home of inflationists and silver-lunatics.

The undisguised truth is that every free silver coinage man is, in reality, an enemy to the best interests of Colorado. When this is clearly understood, the business men—the banking men, the real estate men, the wage-workers and all not blinded by the supposed interests of silver mining, will arise in their might and strangle this most injurious, most dangerous, most noxious delusion. Then will follow a serious effort to expand our silver coinage within the limits of safety, and to reach a true beneficent bimetallism based on a ratio of international agreement.

THE SILVER QUESTION.

A REPLY TO A "PAPER," BY THE HON. CHARLES S. THOMAS OF DENVER.

When I suggested to the Monday Evening Club to invite Hon. Charles S. Thomas to read a paper to it on "The Silver Question," I coupled my suggestion with the remark that, in my opinion, he was the ablest advocate of "Free Silver Coinage" in the State of Colorado. I was anxious that we should hear the strongest and the best that could be offered on that side of this momentous question. To Mr. Thomas' high intellectual qualities, clear expression, forceful style, wide information and brilliant wit, I gladly pay tribute. Nor am I ignorant of the fact that neither in grace of diction nor in any measure of ability can I make compare. And yet in no wise do I fear the conflict because I cherish the trust that the Truth, coming even from a mediocre mind, carries its own pervasive, persuasive force. You can barricade your mind against the truth just as you can barricade your room against the light. But if you are willing to receive the truth—if you will throw open the casement, fling back the curtains, the light will enter and by its own inherent, magical force, will expel the darkness.

Before attacking the question at issue, I want to call attention to one significant fact in the "paper" of Mr. Thomas. He assaults my arguments, conclusions, etc., but he does not, because he cannot, dispute the correctness of a single fact or figure I have quoted. I mention this merely to impress upon your mind that it is a man of truth who is writing this. My reasoning may be lacking in logic, my conclusions may be all astray. That is for you to judge. But the facts and figures I have given and now give have been verified with the most painstaking and most scrupulous care.

One of my critics imputes to me "a sublime innocence of economic understanding." It may be so. I shall not dispute it. Yet despite my sublime folly, I have the conviction that a very brief trial of free and unlimited silver coinage would prompt every man in Colorado to say, in Shakespeare's phrase: "I had rather have a fool to make me merry than experience to make me sad."

Not so very many men in the State would be more benefited by silver rising to $1.29 an ounce than would the writer of this paper. Yet I realize that my desires and my interests can neither warp the logic of cold, hard facts nor twist the effects of irresistible natural laws. Often, when standing on high towers or lofty buildings, I have felt how delightful it would be to jump off and, birdlike, fly slowly down to *terra firma*. I know, however, that the only way to get down is to take the elevator or the stair-case. If I saw that a friend, at my side, misjudging the height, or for any reason, was preparing to leap over, I should feel compelled to take him by the arm and to tell him that it might be pleasant to get down quickly by a plunge in the air, but that the inevitable consequences would be that he would break his neck. If a quick leap into free and unlimited silver coinage would land us safely and permanently on a $1.29 silver *terra firma*, I should want to be one of the first to make the leap. But knowing how Nature works, how inexorable her laws, how pitiless when pitted against foolhardy ventures, I cannot help telling my neighbors in the State that free coinage would be a leap to our own inevitable destruction.

THE TWO DOCTORS.

Whenever I listen to or read the utterances of a clever free silver advocate, I find that, for a considerable distance, I can travel with him in perfect accord. When he contends that, owing to legislation, the purchasing power of gold, has, in a measure, appreciated, I agree with him. When he maintains that one great cause is the world's demonetization of silver, I agree with him. When he maintains that the remedy lies in the world's remonetizing silver, I agree with him. But when he goes a step further and contends that the way to bring it about is for the United States, ALONE AND REGARDLESS OF THE OTHER NATIONS, to open its mint to the free coinage of the world's silver—then our paths immediately and absolutely diverge.

We are like two physicians, met in consultation over a patient. The diagnosis has been made.

Doctor A.—"It is my judgment that our friend has typhoid fever."

Doctor B.—"That is my judgment also."

Doctor A.—"It is my opinion that the cause is the neglected cesspool."

Doctor B.—"That is my opinion also."

Dotor A.—"I should advise giving the patient some quinine."

Doctor B.—"I endorse your judgment absolutely."

Doctor A.—"I propose writing a prescription for an immediate dose of 200 grains of quinine."

Doctor B. (In consternation)—"Two HUNDRED GRAINS?"

Doctor A.—"Yes, sir. I believe in FREE AND UNLIMITED QUININE."

Now, there's the rub. I am willing to grant that the nations are suffering from gold fever. I grant that the cause is a lack of silver in the financial blood. I grant that the remedy needed is to inject more silver into their circulation. But when, instead of distributing the dose to a number of nations, it is proposed to force it down the throat of a single patient, then I maintain that it will produce capitalistic nausea, industrial vomiting, financial paralysis.

THE GREAT "CONSPIRACY" OF 1873.

Free silver men, judging by the importance they give to it, evidently think that the gist of the silver problem rests in the question as to whether silver was demonetized in 1873 by a conspiracy or not. It really has little relevancy. It is harped upon only to inflame passion. I cannot stop to re-discuss the history of that measure. But if there is a man in the United States who seriously has any doubts as to the publicity and cleanness of that legislation, I earnestly beg him to enclose ten cents to Mr. J. H. Hickox, Washington, D. C., dealer in congressional documents, for a copy of the speech delivered by the Hon. A. S. Hewitt in the House of Representatives Aug. 5, 1876. That speech was delivered only three years after the demonetization act. I need say nothing as to the unimpeachable character of Mr. Hewitt. Read that speech attentively, and if you do not rise from its perusal with the conviction that this talk of "conspiracy" is an unfounded, shameless invention, then no further argument of mine on the subject would avail.

Two things, however, I want to call attention to in connection with the Act of 1873. First, it is generally believed that little or no silver was coined after 1873 and until 1878 when the Bland-Allison bill became a law. The report of "The Director of the Mint" shows that more silver was coined between 1873 and up to the date of the Bland-Allison law, than had been coined FOR EIGHTEEN YEARS PREVIOUS. It shows that if we add to this sum the silver trade dollars, which were minted in the same interval, we actually coined MORE SILVER IN THOSE FIVE YEARS THAN

48   THE QUESTION OF SILVER.

FOR THIRTY YEARS PREVIOUS. There was no shortage of silver after 1873. The shortage was the difference between $1.15 an ounce which silver was worth in 1876 and $1.29 which the silver men wanted for that ounce. It was that shortage which in 1876 suddenly led to the discovery of the conspiracy of 1873.

The second point I wish to touch on in connection with the Act of 1873, I introduce by quoting the following lines from Mr. Thomas' " Paper :" " It was about this time that Ernest Seyd, the English banker, made his famous visit to America. Its object has recently been the theme of much discussion, and is therefore familiar to you."

What is the object attributed to Mr. Seyd's visit in 1873? I heard the charge for the first time in " The Denver Mining Congress." It was lately re-told at length in a Denver journal, and is now making the rounds of the Western press. The story is to the effect that in 1873 some English and Continental bankers raised a fund of $500,000 which was given to Mr. Seyd with which to bribe members of Congress in behalf of the object so successfully accomplished in the interest of "the gold ring," to-wit, the crafty demonetization of silver. The only testimony which is given is the following :

"When Congressman Hooper introduced that bill he said: 'Mr. Ernest Seyd of London, a distinguished writer who has given great attention to the subjects of mints and coinage, after reading the first draught of the bill, furnished many valuable suggestions, which have been incorporated in this bill. The committee take no credit for themselves for the preparation of this bill.'"

The story is founded on this testimony.

Now suppose, my reader, that you were walking in a graveyard. You approach the grave of a man whom you had never known, but of whose life and character you had heard report from various reliable sources. A wide sweep of testimony, that had come to you, had brought the conviction that the man at whose grave you were standing, had been the embodiment of honor and rectitude. Of your own knowledge, you knew of his unselfish, self-sacrificing devotion to the support of one particular family which had sadly needed support. While standing in thought, you are suddenly startled to notice that a headboard has been fastened to the grave, inscribed with the foul inscription :

"The man who rests here was a briber, a falsifier and a hypocrite."

And underneath, with still greater horror, you observe that this foul charge is signed with the names of some of the very family for whom he had done so much. What would you do?

You would tear the headboard from its place with an execration on the defamers. That is what I propose to do for the memory of Ernest Seyd.

Note, in the first place, in what a peculiar position this Seyd slander leaves the free silver men. All the free coinage men, who were members of the Congress of 1873, including those who, like Senator Stewart, voted for the demonetization act, have loudly declaimed that they did not know that the act would demonetize silver. And yet now we are told that there was an European envoy there with half a million of "boodle" in his pockets to accomplish this very act. It is hard to understand. As quoted before, ex-Senator Ingalls, a free silver man, could not understand the universal nescience of 1873, except upon the theory that they were all hypnotized. Now if we accepted the "Seyd" theory, one would be led to a suspicion as to what it was that threw them all into the hypnotic state.

But how about the above-quoted remarks of Congressman Hooper? Are not these remarks the very strongest evidence against the slander? If Mr. Seyd had been there with "boodle," wouldn't Mr. Hooper most naturally have suppressed the mention of his name? How came Mr. Seyd there? I do not know. Most likely, the congressional committee invited his attendance. Three years thereafter, the most prominent free silver men, Senators Jones and Bogy, Congressman Bland, with others, were members of "The Silver Commission." On the second page of their report, I find the following:

"Several gentlemen in Europe, eminent as financial authorities, have addressed communications to the commission, which are among the submitted papers. One of these gentlemen, Mr. Cernuschi, appeared personally before the commission, and furnished important and reliable information. The thanks of the country are due to him and to the other distinguished citizens of foreign nations who have made these disinterested efforts in the elucidation of a question important to the welfare of mankind."

Why not now, on the same evidence, concoct the slander that the bankers of France sent Mr. Cernuschi here to bribe our Congress in favor of free silver coinage? The Silver Commission of 1876, composed of senators and congressmen who had all been members of Congress in 1873, made a most impassioned plea for free silver—its report in all, covers a thousand pages—and yet strangely enough, not one word as to the half a million which

Mr. Seyd is now said to have distributed only three years before. Still more strangely, this very Silver Commission instructs our then United States minister to England, Mr. Pierrepont, to obtain Mr. Seyd's answers to certain interrogations, and Mr. Seyd's letter, covering twenty-nine pages, is printed in that Silver Commission report. WHY? Who was Mr. Seyd? Mr. Seyd was an English banker, a man of means and widely known as an author on finance. He was a BIMETALLIST, and the most zealous champion for and BEST FRIEND OF SILVER that England has produced in this century. Long before 1873 and until his death in 1881, he earnestly preached to the European nations the necessity and the advantage of opening their mints to the free coinage of silver.

At the Paris International Conference of 1881 the United States was represented by Mr. Evarts, Mr. Thurman, Mr. Howe and Mr. Dana Horton. Mr. Horton was, in my opinion, by far the ablest bimetallist that has made a study of the subject in the United States. At the fifth session of that conference Mr. Horton, after commenting on the death of the eminent Swiss financier, Mr. Feer-Herzog, said:

"I cannot, however, now pass to our discussion

without having mentioned another occurrence of a similar nature. I speak of the death of Mr. Ernest Seyd, the monetary writer, whose works are known to you, and which took place at Paris since the convening of our conference. It was the profound interest which he took in the conference which brought him here and which, I believe, HASTENED HIS DEATH. How intense that interest was may be well understood when we remember that but a very few years have passed since the day when there was no serious opposition to the general adoption of the gold standard, EXCEPT ON THE PART OF PROFESSOR WOLOWSKI AT PARIS, AND OF ERNEST SEYD, AT LONDON."

And this is the man who, in fact, sacrificed his life in the cause of silver, whom the friends of silver to-day are vilifying as a hired briber. Gentlemen, it must be a very weak cause which resorts to such methods. You should apologize for this slander.

"The nimble lie
Is like the second-hand upon a clock;
We see it fly; while the hour-hand of Truth
Seems to stand still, and yet it moves unseen,
And wins, at last, for the clock will not strike,
Till it has reached the goal."

SUPPLY AND DEMAND.

I have defended the memory of this man, a total stranger to me, as I hope some unknown soul may possibly defend my memory when the grave has made me defenseless. Let us take another look at the question of the production of the money metals. It has been said, in reply to my former "Paper," that if the increased supply of silver depreciated its price, how is it that the enormously increased supply of gold between 1851 and 1870—only depreciated gold but 3 per cent. If my recollection serves me, I said in my "Paper" that the value of the money metals, as of everything else which is given free play, was regulated not by the law of supply—but by the law of supply AND DEMAND. I call attention to the following facts; all, remember, anterior to the demonetization of silver. In the years from 1841 to 1850 the average annual world production of gold and silver was nearly equal in value, viz. 52 per cent. gold, 47 per cent. silver. Unless disturbed by any unequal demand, one would conclude that the ounce price of silver must have been very stable in those ten years.

Such was the fact. In the eight years, 1842–1849, the average annual ounce price of silver never varied one-third of one cent from $1.30. In the next five years, 1851–1855, gold value production was 77 per cent.—silver 22 per cent. Accordingly, as might have been expected, for the average of those five years the silver ounce price rose to $1.34.

The next five years, 1856–1860, the proportion of gold and silver production remained the same as for the previous five years, 77 per cent. and 22 per cent. One would, therefore, naturally expect the silver ounce price to remain the same. But it does not. Its average for these five years is $1.35. The trained observer would then at once conclude that there must have been some increased DEMAND in those second five years. And so it proves. In the five years, 1851–1855, India absorbed fifty-nine millions of silver. In the years 1856–1860, it absorbed two hundred and fifty-one millions. And this silver demand, in spite of relative equal production, would have driven the silver price much higher, if in those same five years, India had not also increased its demand for gold to eighty millions from twenty-seven millions of the previous five-year period.

	Average relative percentage of world's gold production in value.	Average relative percentage of world's silver production in value.	Average price of an ounce of silver.
1861-1856..	72 per cent.	27 per cent.	$1.34
1865-1970..	69 per cent.	30 per cent.	1.32-9

Notice, how, with the rise in the percentage of silver production, the ounce price of silver falls, and this, please remember, was all previous to any demonetization of silver by any of the nations. The fact is that after the enormous increase in the gold production, silver reached its high water mark, $1.36, in 1859. From that year, with slight oscillation, it had fallen to $1.32 in 1870. The laws of supply and demand were steadily forcing it down. That tendency was one of the reasons for demonetization. Now observe, that with an average relative world increase of production from 27 to 30 per cent., the silver ounce price fell 1 1-10 cents. In 1873, the year of our demonetization, the relative percentages stood: Gold 54 per cent., silver 46 per cent. Silver had fallen to $1.29 an ounce. Last year, the relative percentages were reversed—silver 54 per cent. gold 46 per cent. So that, under all circumstances, if there had been no demonetization, it is safe to conclude that silver would to-day be considerably below $1.29 an ounce. It certainly would not without demonetization have stood nearly as low as it stands at present, because demonetization MEANS A DECREASE OF DEMAND. And this decrease of demand is unfortunately contemporaneous with an increase of supply. So I repeat that, with these stolid facts staring one in the face, it would seem to me much easier for the inhabitants of Salt Lake City to bail out their great inland sea with a sieve than that free silver coinage by the United States alone could raise silver to a parity with gold at a ratio of 16:1.

The difference as to gold was that its increased supply came contemporaneously with an enlarged demand both for gold and for the silver that it displaced. All the nations of Europe widely opened their doors to the increasing stock production of gold just as they now have closed them to the increasing production of silver. None the less, gold would relatively have fallen considerably in price if the displaced silver had not during those years found a purchaser. India, by an accidental concurrence of circumstances—large demands for breadstuffs caused by the Crimean war, the temporary exaggeration of the demand for, and the increased price of Indian cotton caused by our rebellion, the Bengal famine, the construction of vast railroad and canal systems, etc., etc.,—caused a demand for silver and gold which was unprecedented. The extent of this money demand will be appreciated when I state that from 1850 to 1875 inclusive, India absorbed of silver and gold the vast sum of over $1,300,000,000,—nearly as much as the entire world's production of silver and gold had been for the thirty years previous—equal in value to the entire stock of gold and silver now held by

England and Germany. This extraordinary Indian demand it was that made the value of gold so comparatively unfluctuating in spite of excessive supply.

THE FARMER AND HIS OXEN.

I am told as a reason for free coinage that silver is more stable than gold as a measure of value. It has been stated that the same amount of gold would now buy two or even three bushels of wheat where it would have bought only one bushel before silver demonetization. It is my opinion also, that gold has appreciated, but by no means in the proportion estimated. Every one knows that the improvement in agricultural machinery of the last twenty years and more especially the improved facilities in the transportation of agricultural products would undoubtedly have contributed to reduce the price of cereals independent of all other conditions. And yet we find the following facts: Taking the average of the years 1869, 1870, 1871— before silver was demonetized—it cost $1.33 gold to buy a bushel of wheat. Taking the average of 1889, 1890, 1891, that same $1.33 would buy not quite one and one-half bushels.

Other influences, much more potent than the appreciation of gold, regulate the price of wheat. In 1860, a bushel of wheat cost within 5 cents of what it cost in 1891,—in 1859 within 2 cents.

The amount of gold that will exchange for an amount of wheat is regulated by the supply of and demand for that gold as compared with the supply of that wheat and the demand for it. If the supply of gold is decreasing with an increased demand, which I take to be the case at present, gold is getting somewhat more than its former equivalent in exchange. If, as I believe, the supply of silver is increasing with a diminished demand, it is sure to get less than its former equivalent in exchange,—provided, always, of course, that the laws of supply and demand have not affected the exchange value of the former equivalent. So that, as a measure of value, silver would be just as unstable on the down grade as gold on the up grade.

A farmer had two oxen. Owing to color and peculiarity of breeding, he called one his "gold ox," the other his "silver ox." He had worked them separately, but had concluded that the "gold ox" walked too quickly and the "silver ox" too slowly. So, like a sensible man, he reasoned that if he yoked them together, the speed of the one would be counteracted by the slow step of the other and thus the average gait would be about right. Now, these oxen had a great antipathy each for the other. The farmer caught the "gold ox" and put the yoke over his neck. By that time the "silver ox" had wandered off. He found him and brought him back, but as he came nearer and nearer, the "gold ox" kept moving off further and further. After unsuccessfully trying to bring them together he unyoked the "gold ox," again caught the "silver ox" and yoked him. Meanwhile the "gold ox" had scampered off. He chased and caught him, led him back, but again the nearer and nearer he brought him to the "silver ox," the further the "silver ox" would move away. So finally, after much loss of time and wear of shoe leather, he was forced to give it up. Then he remembered that most of his farmer neighbors owned the same breed of oxen and he decided to find out how they managed. When he got to his first neighbor, he was told that the same trouble had been experienced. The neighbor had also tried to yoke them together and failed. The same story was repeated by the next neighbor, and the next, and the next. Finally, our original farmer suggested that they all meet early the next morning, and unitedly try to yoke the oxen for each farmer. This was done. They met, yoked the "gold ox," several of the neighbors held him while the others brought in the "silver ox," then they yoked him also, and soon each farmer was getting a good day's even work from both. This illustrates pretty well. Gold alone measures too high. Silver alone measures too low. We must yoke them together, but the United States alone could not do it. We must get the other nations to join and all help yoke together. That is INTERNATIONAL BIMETALLISM.

BIMETALLIC FRANCE.

Mr. Thomas says:

"It is asserted that the debtor will be disappointed because with the free and unlimited coinage of silver there will be an immediate and total disappearance of gold. This is the stale repetition of one of the stalest of platitudes against the free and unlimited coinage of silver. It is refuted by all the facts of history. Bimetallic France is a living illustration of its falsity * * * There never was and never will be a nation using a standard based upon both the metals, priced at a proper equilibrium, which will suffer in the manner indicated by this objection."

It must have been observed that a free silver man is never so completely happy as when, with uplifted arm, he says, "Look at bimetallic France!" Let us, accordingly, take a look at her financial history, briefly told. It will teach many lessons. Among others it will teach something more about Gresham's law. We are told that the cause of the disappearance of silver in the United States after 1834 was not due to Gresham's law, because "the operation of that law applies to a debased coinage, as compared with a standard one." I am willing to leave judgment on that point to any reader who has ever received even kindergarten instruction in political economy. Free silver men don't like Gresham's law and I don't blame them. I have never fallen down-stairs without feeling that the law of gravitation was a nuisance.

Now for France. In 1726, the ratio of gold to silver was placed at 1:14⅝. An ounce of gold was worth more than 4⅝ ounces of silver, and consequently, gold soon disappeared from circulation. Adam Smith, having visited France in 1764, said: "It is there difficult to get more gold than what is necessary to carry in your pocket." M. Calonne, who became the French minister of state in 1783, wrote: "Everybody knows that hardly any more gold was to be seen in France and that it had become infinitely scarce in Paris." In 1785, Louis the Sixteenth, in an edict, calls attention to the fact that the legal ratio of gold to silver differing from the commercial ratio, had as to the gold coins "originated the speculation of selling them to the foreigner, and offers the temptation of a great profit to those who may allow themselves to melt them down." He then ordains that "every gold mark of 24 carats fine shall be worth 15½ marks of silver 12 deniers fine." This established the French ratio of 15½:1 still existing.

In 1790 the revolutionists had control of France. They had confiscated the lands of the clergy the year before. They wanted money. So they conceived the ingenious idea of using paper money, which they called ASSIGNATS, basing their value on these confiscated lands. In April they issued 400 millions of francs in assignats. In September 800 millions more. This they declared would be the last issue. The assignats worked beautifully. Everybody received and exchanged them at full value. Then some one said, just as the greenback inflationists said in the seventies and just as silver men say now: "If this franc is as good as any other franc, how can we have too many of them? The law makes the value of money." So the presses were set to work, and within a few years they had issued over forty-five billions of those paper francs. The Government seemed surprised that any one should make a difference between a coin franc and a paper franc—and a law was passed that any one making such a difference in trade should be imprisoned for six years. They could jail individuals but they couldn't jail natural laws. No one would exchange one coin franc for less than nearly 300 paper francs. Then in 1796 these political economists tried another experiment. They cut up the confiscated lands into exact parcels, exchanged the ASSIGNATS at about 3 per cent. of their face value for what they called MANDATS, and proclaimed that the holder of mandats could select any parcel of this land and pay in mandats. Within a few months the mandats were worth one-seventieth of their face value, and they were soon, with great and universal financial suffering, wiped out altogether.

In 1803 the ratio of 15½ : 1 was reënacted. M. Chevalier, the eminent French economic authority, writes :

"In the year 1803, when the ratio of 1 : 15½ between the metals was established, this ratio actually existed in the commercial world; but little by little it changed, and soon gold came to be worth ordinarily a little more than 15½ times as much as silver. This discrepancy sufficed to retire gold from circulation. A few years after the passage of the law of 1803, gold became so scarce that people had to buy it of the money-changers when they wanted to carry that kind of cash on their journeys. In fact the circulation of the two metals side by side had ceased to exist shortly after the year 1803, and twenty-five years after that date the circulation consisted of silver only."

Sir G. B. Airy, the Royal Astronomer of England, wrote:

"In the year 1826, I spent some time in France. The gold coin was a little too rich, and no gold coin could be got. The better class of farmers went to market followed by their servants, who carried huge bags of five franc pieces. In 1829, I again passed through France; I wished for gold, and obtained it by paying a heavy premium."

In 1848 came the increased production of gold in Russia, in 1849 in California, in 1851 in Australia. Silver soon rose to a value higher than $15\frac{1}{2}:1$ and, consequently, silver rushed out of France at such a rate that a commission even reported the advisability of placing an export duty on silver. Some idea can be formed of the vast influx of gold, when I state that from 1795 to 1850 France coined four times more silver than gold; whereas, from 1850 to 1872, she coined eight times more gold than silver. Early in the '60s, Gresham's law had pushed out from France even the fractional silver coins to such an extent that it became a great public inconvenience. Investigation showed that Belgium and Switzerland were similarly troubled; correspondence followed, and the result was the organization in 1865, of The Latin Monetary Union, comprising France, Belgium, Switzerland and Italy. Later, Greece also became a member. All these countries use the franc system of money. They agreed on a basis of silver coinage, reducing the metallic value of the subsidiary coins.

After 1859, silver had again taken the downward course which has characterized its value through the centuries. In 1867, at the International Monetary Conference held at Paris under the presidency of Prince Napoleon, it was decided, without a dissenting vote, that gold should be the sole money standard. The spirit of silver demonetization was abroad. Silver had been out of circulation so long in the United States that Mr. Ruggles, the American delegate, in reply to a question of Prince Napoleon, said: "Though the double standard still exists legislatively in the United States, it is virtually abolished in practice, and hence the United States has the gold standard alone." In 1871, after the Franco-German war, Germany decided to place itself on the gold standard, and to demonetize silver. Between 1873 and 1879 Germany sold $140,000,000 of her silver. The neighboring countries which up to that time, had always maintained the free and unlimited coinage of gold and silver, became alarmed at the threatened influx of silver and expulsion of gold. So in 1874 the Latin Union met, and from that year on there has been no free and unlimited coinage of silver in France, Belgium, Switzerland and Italy. They LIMITED the coinage of silver. And in 1878 THEY STOPPED THE COINAGE OF LEGAL TENDER SILVER *in toto*, so that for thirteen years our much applauded bimetallic France has not coined a single legal tender silver coin. If the example of bimetallic France is a good one to follow, then our whole silver legislation since 1878 has been a grand mistake. Since 1878 France has only coined a limited amount of fractional silver coin. Last year the silver coinage of England was over $8,000,000. How much, O ye silver men! was the whole year's silver coinage of bimetallic France? THREE HUNDRED THOUSAND DOLLARS. Less than the United States is putting into silver money EVERY TWO DAYS. There is not much consolation in the example of France for a free silver advocate. Let us close this branch of the subject by the following quotations. I preface them by saying that M. Cernuschi of Paris was a recognized master in the domain of political economy and the most passionate bimetallist and most eager advocate for reintroduction of silver as a money metal that this century has produced. He fought for silver AS A KNIGHT FIGHTS FOR HIS LADY.

Place, Washington: Time, 1876: Scene: Committee-room of "The Silver Commission." Questions are put by the chairman:

"*Question.* If we stand in the presence of great nations like Germany and China, which do not have the double standard, and when we see another great country like England, whose ancient prejudices or reasons, whatever they may be, will not allow her to consent in our time or in the near future to the adoption of bimetallism, must we forego the advantages which bimetallism offers until these nations can grow up to that position in which they can adopt it, or until their prejudices can be overcome?

"*M. Cernuschi.* It requires great audacity.

"*Question.* Then I ask you whether it requires more audacity than was required on the part of France when, singly and alone, she boldly took the step, and without a union with any other country, succeeded in maintaining the variation intact and to her own great advantage for sixty-five or seventy years ; I ask whether at this time, when we have the assistance of France, when we have the Latin Union formed and have a knowledge concerning money much in advance of that which obtained when France formed the relation, we cannot adopt it with much more assurance of success than had France at the time of her adoption of it?

"*M. Cernuschi.* But France was not then in the presence of a country demonetizing silver. She had not to restore silver and to invent the bimetallism.

SILVER WAS THE PRINCIPAL MONEY IN EUROPE. France acted with her forces and SHE HAD NOT TO FIGHT AGAINST THE FORCES OF THE OTHERS.

"*Question.* Now I ask could not France herself, assisted by the States of the Latin Union, take the silver which Germany has to offer as well as any surplus from the mines over and above the demands of the rest of the world and thus maintain the parity between silver and gold, as she did formerly, in the presence of a large supply of gold?

"*M. Cernuschi.* The position of France is not at present what it was before 1871. Then France had on one side England, (monometallic gold), on the other side Germany, (monometallic silver). Being bimetallic herself it was easy and usual for her to be changing the coinage of the two metals. To-day all is different. If France coins silver, ALL THE SILVER OF THE WORLD, beginning with the German silver, WOULD FLOW INTO FRANCE."

A disgusted spirit-voice is heard from the Far West: "Confound this bimetallic France."

MORE MONEY.

One cry is that we need more money. What is money? Money is a medium of exchange, a measure of value, and a standard of deferred payment. What makes money? The imprint or the stamp (virtually the signature) of the Government makes the money, but that does not make the value of the money. Every bit of coin or paper money issued is a check for its face value made payable to bearer and signed by the Government. If I fill out a number of checks for say ten dollars each, make them payable to bearer, and sign them, those checks will pass where I am known and where it is thought that my bank account will redeem those checks. But if any doubt arises, if the bank refuses payment on any of my checks, then they will be no longer circulate at face value, but may be taken at some lower value proportional to the chances of my paying them up in the future. Government checks or money are subject to the same law. During our war, the Government stamped its signature on some green paper and called it a dollar. Yet there was a doubt whether the Government would ever give a full gold dollar for those "greenbacks," and therefore in 1865 they were worth about sixty-seven cents. The Confederate government also stamped bills "one dollar," but there were times when it took a hundred Confederate dollars to buy a five-cent Seidlitz powder. Why? The signature was all right but the credit behind that signature was all wrong. With paper money or with all money that has not a full intrinsic metallic value, it is the credit of the Government that makes the value. My last sentence indicates a difference. If you happen to drop a five dollar gold piece into the fire it melts, but if you take out the molten mass it is still worth five dollars. In other words, the material out of which the check is made is worth the five dollars with or without the signature. If anyone handling one of my checks made payable to bearer, should bring it near a lighted candle, set it on fire and burn off my signature, the check has no value except the infinitesimal value of the bit of paper still left unconsumed. If by accident I drop a silver dollar in the fire and pick out the molten mass, it will be worth no longer a dollar, but only seventy-three cents. Why? Because the signature has been destroyed. Now because the Government, by affixing its signature to that seventy-three cents worth of metal makes it worth 100 cents, is no reason why the miners of that metal should be entitled to that difference of twenty-seven cents. A nickel is a government check for five cents. Melt it, erase the signature, and it is worth one-half cent. Would it not now be just as reasonable for the miners of nickel to ask free and unlimited coinage for that metal so that they could make a difference of 4½ cents on every five cent piece?

"But why," I am repeatedly asked, "does the seventy-three cent dollar circulate as well and buy as much as a 100-cent dollar?" You and I and every other citizen take the silver dollar as readily as the gold dollar because we can exchange it readily for a gold dollar. The bank you deposit with, if you indicate a preference, will exchange the silver dollar for a gold dollar. That bank can send the silver dollars to its correspondent-bank in the East and again exchange for gold dollars. That Eastern bank can send the silver to the treasury of the United States and obtain gold dollars in even exchange. It is always the credit of the Government behind it and the Government's implied guarantee that it will exchange one for the other. How is it that the Government can make the exchange? Because the coinage of silver is LIMITED. If it were UNLIMITED, then after the gold had gone out of the treasury, the treasury could no longer exchange for the Eastern bank, the Eastern bank no longer exchange for the home bank, the home bank no longer exchange for its customer, and the customer in his dealings would make a difference between the gold dollar and the silver dollar—and gold would at once be at a premium.

What is money good for? It has little value in itself. It is good to be exchanged for money's worth. So that a man's wealth does not depend upon the money he owns. A man wrecked on a desert island might have a billion dollars of gold and silver and yet be a very poor devil. England has more wealth per capita than we have—although we have considerably more money per capita than England has.

One of the great delusions about money is the "per capita" delusion. Silver men are always quoting the fact that France has $44.55 per capita circulation while we have only $24.38. They always forget to add that England has only $18.60 per capita circulation and Germany only $18.02. Is there any advantage in having a large per capita circulation? Certainly not. If $24.38 is enough to do our business exchange properly, it would be folly to have a penny more. A disproportionately large "per capita" stock of money in circulation in any nation is prima facie evidence that the people of that nation are backward in civilization so far as the art of using money and credit is concerned. That is true of France. Every one knows of the hoarding propensity of the French peasant. Banks are very scarce in France. Frenchmen know comparatively little of the convenience of banks. I lived in France the greater part of five years. We kept house, and my expenses were large. Yet in those five years I never issued and never received a check. Naturally, in a country in which such financial methods prevail, the money-circulation per capita must be extremely large. It is safe to predict that, as France more and more partakes of the benefits of extended banking facilities, its per capita circulation of money will, just in that proportion, decrease.

"Yes, but England in her late financial troubles drew on bimetallic France for fifteen millions of gold." I know she did, and I also know that England lately, in her troubles, drew on bimetallic United States for over sixty millions of gold. If France hadn't prohibited free silver coinage in 1874 SHE WOULDN'T HAVE HAD THE GOLD TO SEND. It is worth noting also that French rentes bearing 3 per cent. interest are quoted at 90 while English 2¾ per cent. consols are quoted above par.

Yet still the silver voice replies "MORE MONEY." Let me quote a sentence from a speech of the Hon. Judge Belford delivered before the Transmississippi Congress in Denver last May:

"The currency of this country has been diminished hundreds of thousands of dollars since the conclusion of the hostilities that existed between the respective sections of the country, and the discontent to which I have alluded is the direct result of the constant curtailment of the currency of the people, and the diminution of the means by which their domestic and foreign commerce is carried on."

The hostilities between the respective sections of the country concluded in 1865. The report of the secretary of the treasury shows that in 1865 we had a money stock of 745,000,000 with 714,000,000 in circulation. In 1891 we had money stock of TWENTY-ONE HUNDRED MILLIONS with over FIFTEEN HUNDRED MILLIONS in circulation. The year 1860 was a very prosperous year. Compare its monetary condition with 1891, July 1, of each year.

	Population.	General money stock.	Money in circulation.	Per capita circulation.
1860..	31,500,000	442,000,000	435,000,000	$15.85
1891..	64,000,000	2,100,000,000	1,500,000,000	23.45

This shows that, with all the improvements we have made in facilitating exchanges, by means of banks, clearing-houses, telegraph, etc., etc., we have, while DOUBLING our population, increased our money stock FIVE-FOLD. In the name of the silver moon, when are we going to have money enough to satisfy this class of economists? Attention should be called to the fact that from 1860 to 1878 inclusive, the difference between our total money stock and the money in circulation seldom exceeded 10 per cent. The difference has been widening since 1878, until to-day it is over 40 per cent. That would indicate to me that we already had much more money than the business of the country required.

Any one who knows anything about our business methods understands that all our business is done with—making the proportions very conservative—10 per cent. of money and 90 per cent. of confidence. So plenty of confidence is worth nine times as much as plenty of money. Last November, a year ago, money, with the best securities, was worth 180 per cent. per annum in New York. Two months, thereafter, it was worth 2½ per cent. per annum. What made the difference? Confidence. Take our present time. Our country never had so much money. Yet money is close. The banks are not inclined to make long loans. Why? Lack of confidence. What causes that? The silver agitation. Prominent silver men have admitted it in Congress. But they say that it is only the suspense before realization, that after free coinage is established all will be well.

A jailer enters the cell of a man condemned to death and finds him exceedingly depressed. He says, "Cheer up, man! It is only the suspense that's unpleasant. After you have dangled a few minutes, it will all be over." The reply would probably be: "Thank you!

This suspense is hard to bear, but if you can get the governor to prolong the suspense a few years, I shall appreciate it."

To repeat, we need not more money, but more confidence. In fact, if the free silver agitators were to reduce our money volume by 33 per cent. and by holding their peace, would give us a feeling of confidence, of security and of financial safety, every business man in the country would have reason to feel extremely obliged.

THE NEGLECTED " BIG BONANZA."

We are told that England, for her selfish profit, keeps the gold standard for herself and the silver standard for her dependencies. Evidently these declaimers are ignorant of the fact that England has repeatedly desired to put India on a gold standard, but has had to give way to the prejudices of her Indian subjects in favor of silver.

We are told: "England buys her silver of us at 95 cents an ounce, coins it into rupees at a profit of 36 cents per ounce, exchanges it at par for Indian wheat, and then sells this wheat at Liverpool at prices which govern the value of our surplus product, which in turn fixes the price for it all." Please read that again. It is one of the most marvelous statements made in behalf of the free silver cause. Senator Stewart, Senator Tabor and the other financial and literary headlights of that party have repeated it. The American farmer has been hoodwinked and inflamed by it.

I always thought that we were a nation of shrewd business men, but the above statement forces me to believe that we are a pack of dough-heads. Understand, please, that England does not coin the rupees, that the mints at Calcutta and Bombay are open to the free coinage of silver, that these mints will coin your silver and my silver into rupees as readily as the silver of any Englishman, and yet for all these years we have been selling our silver at 95 cents, letting those foxy Englishmen carry it to India, coin it into rupees at a basis of $1.36, buy Indian commodities worth $1.36 in the markets of the world and on every ounce of silver, pocket the difference between 95 cents and $1.36.

Ye Denver smelting men, I thought you were men of business! Yesterday's paper informs me that the product of your smelters for 1891 was over 18,000,000 ounces of silver. You sold that on an average of 98½ cents an ounce. It would not have cost much over 1½ per cent. to send it to India, and then instead of selling it here for ninety-five cents, you might, by buying Indian commodities worth $1.36 and reselling them, have made an additional profit of nearly seven millions of dollars. Let me advise you to get six of these free silver men amply to guarantee the above quoted statement, take them into partnership for your Indian exchange business, give them a salary of half a million a-piece and you will still make nearly four millions additional profit.

The fact is that the merchants of Bombay who deal in exportable commodities are as lynx-eyed as any in the world. They watch and calculate on the slightest fluctuation of silver. When Congress was debating the silver question in 1890 (I have this statement from the ex-United States minister to Turkey), those Indian merchants were listening to every click of the telegraph to guide them in their commercial ventures.

Poor, deluded, bamboozled American farmer! The story is a myth. Free silver or no free silver, India or no India, the price of your wheat is regulated wholly by its supply as compared to the world's demand.

MEXICO AND BIMETALLISM.

Mr. Thomas says: "We are referred to Mexico. She is a silver standard nation. Like all other countries using that standard alone, gold has no place in its financial economy." Now that is pretty smooth, but it is a most damaging admission. The mints of Mexico are open to the free coinage of gold and silver, but the gold doesn't come. However, she " is a silver standard nation." That is what I have been trying to beat into the heads of the free silver men. With free silver coinage, we shall be just what Mexico is to-day, a silver standard nation. Why? Because with us just as it has been in Mexico, the gold would be driven out.

But it is said: "If driven out, where would it go to? Certainly to the gold standard countries. The influx of such a vast quantity of gold into Europe, would make money far more plentiful abroad, prices would rise with the fall of money values, and the operation of the law would of itself not only check, but completely stop its departure."

Mr. Jevons, the eminent political economist, put this theory thus: " Imagine two reservoirs of water, each subject to independent variations of supply and demand. In the absence of any connecting pipe the level of the water in each reservoir will be subject to its own fluctuations only. But if we open a connection, the water in both will assume a certain mean level, and the effect of any excessive supply or demand will be distributed over the whole area of both reservoirs."

This is the theory on which bimetallism rests and can rest its faith. But one most important modification must be made. It holds perfectly good if the capacity of the two reservoirs are equal or approximately equal. But suppose that one of the connected reservoirs has a capacity of five million gallons—the other fifty million gallons. Then comes a storm which floods water in great volume into the fifty million reservoir. It pours a great mass of water into the five million reservoir. Can the compensatory action, the reflow take place until equilibrium is restored? No, the dam of the smaller reservoir breaks and destruction follows. As to bimetallism, it is as with the reservoirs—a question of area. If a sufficient number of nations agree to adopt it, it will be safe. If not, it will be most dangerous.

GOING IT ALONE.

The principle of bimetallism is all right, but the danger consists in "going it alone." This is the vital point. Let me quote on this subject the opinions of the most prominent bimetallists of our century. First, Mr. Francis A. Walker, author of the ablest American work on "Money," professor of Yale college, lecturer of John Hopkins university commissioned as a delegate to the International Monetary Conference of 1878, because of his ability and of his devotion to bimetallism. Before the House committee on January 29, 1891, he said :

"For fourteen years I have been an earnest and consistent advocate of the restoration of silver to its rank as a money metal of full legal tender powers, and there is scarce a political result which is conceivable, likely to take place within any reasonable term of time, which would bring me greater joy than the union of the United States with the principal commercial nations of Europe, in establishing the free coinage of silver upon a common ratio. But the present measure, it seems to me, is a menace to the very object and it is especially as a bimetallist, a consistent and earnest bimetallist, that I have felt called upon to say a word in question of the present measure.

"I confess that I cannot conceive how any man who has largely studied the question can believe, can even hope, that the United States can go it alone in this matter of silver coinage; can undertake to do so without coming to speedy grief and humiliation. I am very well aware that many gentlemen do honestly so hope and so believe, but the overwhelming preponderance of the educated financial opinion of the world inclines to the belief that the proposed measure would simply result in stripping us of our gold, in upsetting our exchanges with the great trading and producing nations of the world, in bringing us down to the level of second-rate financial powers only, such as China, India, and South America, and involving our trade and production in all the evils, the inexpressible evils of a depreciated and fluctuating currency."

I next invoke the testimony of the eminent Henri Cernuschi mentioned before. Testimony before the Silver Commission of 1876:

"*Question.* Why not adopt bimetallism in France, and let Germany do as she pleases?

"*M. Cernuschi.* Because in that case, all the silver would come to France.

"*Question.* In case the United States should resolve to adopt the bimetallic standard at any proportion, say $15\frac{1}{2}:1$, and other countries should maintain their present position with reference to the issue of gold and silver respectively, what, in your opinion, would be the effect upon the business of the country?

"*M. Cernuschi.* My desire is that a general agreement shall be adopted by the different nations. In my opinion NO COUNTRY CAN COIN SILVER ALONE; any country that coins only silver will remain alone and will not have the money for paying abroad.

"*Question.* Would it be necessary for the maintenance of such relative value between the two metals that all the countries establishing that relation should join in a convention?

"*M. Cernuschi.* I do not say that it is necessary to have all the countries, but it would be sufficient to obtain the concurrence of some leading countries."

Next let us listen to words spoken at the International Monetary Conference of 1881.

I preface by stating that an "international monetary conference" is not a "Denver mining congress." Each country sends as delegates two or three of its most distinguished men, its ablest financial representatives. There is no buncombe there. Every man is a deep student of political economy. No delegate dare state an erroneous fact as to the finances of any nation, because right opposite him sits an accredited delegate of that nation who can put him right in the twinkling of an eye. Hence the words spoken at the "international monetary conferences" (of which there have been three—1867, 1878, and 1881) carry the very greatest weight with intelligent thinking men.

At the 1881 conference M. Magnin, the delegate from France, then minister of France, said:

"In order that the metal silver may recover its former value it is indispensable that it should be, as in the past, freely coined side by side with gold, and as no State either wishes to stand, or could stand, alone in resuming such coinage, it is absolutely certain that we shall not find our way out of the present difficulties until an international bimetallic treaty shall have been concluded."

Mr. Pierson, delegate of the Netherlands, said :

"Gresham's law is doubtless opposed to the establishment of the bimetallic system in a small group of States, but not to its establishment on a territory embracing the most civilized countries of the world."

Mr. Forssell, the delegate of Sweden, said :

"It is the opinion, even of the boldest bimetallist, that the obligations corresponding to the salutary liberties of the free mintage of both metals would henceforth be unbearable without the co-operation of all, or of most of the first-class States ; that the heedless State, which would undertake alone the necessary efforts for rehabilitating and sustaining the value of silver, would be crushed under the weight of the bimetallic system, which would at once fall to pieces; that it would be suffocated by the silver flowing in from the whole world."

This needs no further argument. I simply submit to the judgment of my reader whether, in a momentous question of this kind, it is safe to follow the opinion of our Colorado free silver leaders, or the authority of the distinguished men I have quoted.

WILL SILVER ADVANCE TO $1.29 ?

Under free coinage, we are told, silver is going to advance and to be worth permanently $1.29 an ounce. Some maintain that it will be worth even more. The Hon. Mr. Symes of Denver told the "Transmississippi Congress" in May:

"When the United States returns to true bimetallism by free coinage there will be no anxiety as to whether there is a little more or a little less than one hundred millions of gold in the treasury. The bullion value of the silver dollar will be greater than the ratio of the bullion value of the gold dollar."

Let us reason as to this a bit. There is on our planet, in round figures, three billions nine hundred million dollars worth of silver held as money, or as a fund for money redemption. That is to-day all worth about 95 cents an ounce. Now these free silver men tell us that the magical alchemy of free coinage by the United States all alone, is going to raise these thirty-nine hundred millions from 95 cents to $1.29. That is, it is going to add a value of over a BILLION dollars to the world's silver stock. Astounding proposition!

Let us appeal to history: In 1793, as we know, our fathers after a very careful examination of what gold and silver were worth in the world, decided that an ounce of gold was worth fifteen times as much as an ounce of silver, and accordingly fixed the ratio of 15:1. That was on a basis of silver being worth $1.38 an ounce. The United States had free and unlimited coinage. All the other nations had free and unlimited coinage. Yet beginning the very next year, silver was worth a little less than $1.38 an ounce. From 1793 to 1871 (when Germany started silver demonetization)—nearly eighty years—all the nations of the world, except England, held their mints open to the free and unlimited coinage of silver. Yet during that whole period, silver never again rose to our mintage value, $1.38 an ounce. In 1859 it was worth $1.36 an ounce. In 1814 even $1.37½ an ounce. But never again $1.38. Let us take the year 1819. Silver was worth $1.35 an ounce, within three cents of par. The world's stock of money silver was about fifteen hundred millions of dollars. Silver had to rise less than 2¼ per cent. to be par at a ratio of 15:1. The sum necessary to be added to the value of silver to make it reach par was only thirty millions, and yet with free and unlimited coinage all over the world, IT COULD NOT ADD THAT VALUE. And now when the difference between silver and par is not THREE cents but THIRTY-FIVE cents, when silver has to rise not 2¼ per cent. but 35 per cent., when the value to be added to the world's silver is not thirty millions but more than a THOUSAND AND THIRTY millions, some men want us to believe that free silver coinage by the United States alone is going to accomplish it. Can we, in the light of financial history, imagine a more unreasonable statement?

How trustworthy have the statements of the free silver men been in the past as to the rise of silver value? The Silver Commission of 1876 comprised the ablest advocates of a free silver policy. In their report, this commission says: "The tendency of the two metals to return to their old relation, or of silver to recover from its fall, if the latter mode of expression is to any persons more acceptable, was manifested very soon after the silver panic of last July, and has made a degree of progress which tends to confirm the belief that, in any event, the full recovery of the old relation may be relied upon."

Silver then was worth $1.15 an ounce. After this prophecy of 1876—silver has fallen more within the last fifteen years than in two and a half centuries before."

Then came the bill of 1878. That was going to send silver right up. In 1878, ounce price of silver $1.15. In 1879, $1.12. Then came the bill of 1890. President Harrison in a letter to "The Western States Commercial Congress," April 14, 1891, says of this bill:

"The legislation adopted by the first session of the Fifty-first Congress I was assured by leading advocates of free coinage, representatives of the silver States, WOULD PROMPTLY AND PERMANENTLY BRING SILVER TO $1.29 PER OUNCE AND KEEP IT THERE."

Senator Teller's speech in the senate yesterday, Jan. 6,—brought out the noteworthy fact that both Senator Jones and Senator Stewart—the Pope and First Cardinal of The Silver Church—had predicted most positively that the legislation of 1890 would lift silver to $1.29 an ounce.

When the bill passed, the price of the silver ounce was $1.08. To-day it is 95 cents.

It seems to be a reasonable statement that, other things being equal, the force necessary to replace an object must be equal to the force which displaced it. If ten men by exerting all their strength, move a stone weighing two tons a certain distance, is it reasonable to suppose that one man of those ten, using the same tools, can push it back to its starting-point? Since 1871 silver has been demonetized by ten nations. That demonetization, we are told, has driven silver down to its present price. Is it likely that its remonetization by a single one of the ten nations is going to lift it to its former value?

EFFECT ON BIMETALLISM.

The free and unlimited coinage of silver by the United States, independent of international co-operation, will be the expiring gasp of bimetallism. The last opportunity of inducing other nations to join in a free bimetallic movement will be forever lost. No one who has carefully studied the expressions of the most eminent students of finance in Europe, but must have concluded that, in the event of our adopting free silver coinage, Belgium, Switzerland and Austria would at once place themselves absolutely on the single gold standard. My impression is that France would also.

At the "Monetary Conference" of 1878, Mr. Feer-Herzog, the delegate from Switzerland, said: "In Switzerland and Belgium it is hoped that silver, after a period of transition, during which it will only have legal tender for a small sum, may be finally reduced to the simple *rôle* of fractional money. M. De Parieu, delegate of France to the conference of 1867 and its vice-president, wrote to the Silver Commission of 1886 :

"The progressive and intelligent political economists of Europe who are occupied with monetary questions, will therefore be divided between the desire to see America, in the interest of general legislation, keep in the path of its legislation from 1872 to 1876, and that of receiving from her the means of disburdening their national circulation, at the least cost, of the ballast of silver which exceeds what is necessary for a suitable amount of change."

Strange as it may seem, even India might jump to the gold standard. In the 1881 conference Sir Louis Mallet, the delegate from British India, said: "It is certain that if the depreciation of silver continues, and if by reason of the discovery of fresh deposits of gold, or from some other cause, the OPPORTUNITY SHOULD OFFER ITSELF, we should only be too ready to seize it, and to return to the proposals of the commission which sat at Calcutta in 1868 and to enter, though much against our wish, into the struggle which is about to commence between the nations of the earth for the sole metal which will be left to us as the solid basis of an international currency."

THE TEN MINERS.

There has been and is great monetary pressure in Europe. There has been a fierce international struggle for gold. There has been and is a serious financial strain. Every dollar of silver that we have coined since 1878, every dollar that the Government has purchased and stored in its treasury vaults, has just, in that proportion, tended to relieve that strain, and just so far operated against the adoption of international bimetallism. If all the silver in excess of our needs had been sold abroad just as we sold our wheat, our pork and other surplus commodities, silver might have been worth somewhat less per ounce, but we would have more gold, the European nations just so much less gold, and they would have been influenced ere this, to join in an international bimetallic treaty. Certainly, we do not want to rush into free silver coinage now, unload their silver,—give them our gold, and by relieving them of their monetary pressure, make it easy for them to adopt the single gold standard.

There are ten mines on a hillside. All can work and take out ore, but all are greatly troubled by water. It interferes with making their output as large as it ought to be. One of these mines is at a lower level than the others. Every gallon that the owner of that mine pumps out tends, just in that proportion, to drain the other nine mines. He cannot afford to pump out the water for all. He wants the other mine owners to join in that expense. What is his policy? Is it to say:

"I shall keep right on pumping until you

others join with me"? Will that force the others to join? Is it not rather his policy to say firmly: "Not another drop will I pump out until you co-operate with me both in the labor and the expense"?

That is what America, instead of doing all the pumping alone since 1878, should have said to the nations of Europe. The following figures speak volumes to a thinking man:

Total product of silver in the United States for fourteen years from 1865 to 1877, 320,000,000; from 1878 to 1891, 735,000,000. Net excess of exports of silver from the United States for fourteen years from 1865 to 1877, 223,000,000; from 1878 to 1891, 137,000,000. This shows that, owing to our peculiar legislation, with an INCREASE of 130 per cent. in the production of silver for the last fourteen years, there has been a DECREASE in our exports of silver of 39 per cent.

It is very significant that in the year 1891, the second time only in forty-four years, our imports of silver exceeded our exports.

THE AMERICAN FARMER.

If free coinage will not put silver up, it will necessarily put the American silver dollar down—and will the farmer then be happy? If he is a debtor, he will have obtained a proportionate reduction of that debt. But every farmer, as is every man, is to a certain extent a creditor also. His greatest debtor is his land. The farmer lends to his land in the spring and collects the debt at harvest-time. It is important that no discounts be made on that debt. But the speculation which the purchaser of the farm product would have to make as to the rise and fall of silver would operate as a large discount. Our exports of agricultural products for last year were six hundred and forty-two millions. A small discount on that sum every year would be A TERRIBLE LOSS TO THE FARMER.

See how the shifting price of silver affects India. Sir Louis Mallet says:

"It is no doubt true that when trade has been able to adapt itself to an alteration in the relative value of the standards of the two countries, if this alteration was of a permanent character and took place once for all, the evil would cease. But, gentlemen, this is not the case. The future is as uncertain as the present in the existing state of things; and it is this uncertainty which impedes and prevents trade.

"For each commercial operation two calculations are necessary. The price of goods must first be calculated in gold, and the price of gold in silver; and for the latter there is no basis on which to go. It is just as if one had to buy cotton with gold in order to be in a position to buy wheat with cotton. In fact, it is nothing but a kind of primitive barter, worthy only of an early civilization. In my opinion, then trade sustains an evil, and a very serious one."

The farmer's price for his products is regulated by the price he gets for his exportable surplus. The fall of the value of the dollar, caused by free coinage, would make nearly every price rise in proportion to that fall except the prices of the farmer's products. So that the farmer would have to meet the world-competition in price for what he sold, and yet pay an advanced price for everything he purchased. Surely "the last state of that man is worse than the first."

WHY HAVE WE MORE GOLD NOW?

The silver men say: "It was said that the law of 1878 would drive gold out. Why is it that ever since 1878 our gold stock has so rapidly increased?" The coinage of silver has had no effect upon the question, except in so far as our refusal to sell it abroad, just as we sold our wheat, our cotton, etc., HAS REDUCED the gold stock which would otherwise have come to us. The reason of the increase of gold is very simple as shown by the following most extraordinary statement of our foreign trade. For the fourteen years, from 1864 to 1877 inclusive, our IMPORTS exceeded our exports by OVER EIGHT HUNDRED MILLIONS OF

DOLLARS. For the fourteen years, from 1878 to 1891 inclusive, OUR EXPORTS exceeded our imports by OVER FOURTEEN HUNDRED MILLIONS. That balance was paid in gold and hence our increased gold stock since 1878.

GOLD DISAPPEARANCE AND SILVER INUNDATION.

With the free coinage of silver, gold would at once jump to a premium and disappear from circulation. M. Cernuschi, asked in 1876, where the injury would come if we started free coinage, replied: "The injury would be that at the first moment all your gold would disappear." The silver dollar, as compared with gold, would be looked upon as a metallic greenback. Gold disappearance would mean temporary contraction of the money volume and a deadly blow to all enterprise and business.

It would be flashed to all corners of the earth that the people of the United States were willing to pay $1.29 for every ounce of silver. Every ship would come into our harbors laden down with silver. The price of silver would rise, but men of affairs would know that the advance, just like the advance after the bill of 1890, could hold but for a short time.

Where would the silver come from? Outside of the United States, there are about thirty-three hundred million dollars worth of silver. In Europe alone eleven hundred millions. The Bank of France has $250,000,000 in its vaults. Does it need them? In the Monetary Conference of 1881, M. Pirmez, the Belgian delegate, said: "The Bank of France itself has tried to get acceptance for the five-franc pieces it is constantly putting into circulation, but it has failed, and this cumbersome coin is constantly brought back to it." In 1878, Mr. Feer-Herzog, the Swiss delegate, said:

"It is none the less true that this stock of coined silver far exceeds the requirements of the internal circulation of the Latin Union; the people do not like it, and reject it: foreign commerce does not accept these coins at the artificial value attributed to them by law, so that they flow into the public treasuries and great financial establishments, and choke the cellars of the Bank of France.

The following letter was written, (Paris, Dec. 10, 1890) by Mr. William Seligman, brother of Mr. Jesse Seligman, the New York banker now endeavoring to promote bimetallism in Europe:

"Free coinage would be hailed with joy in Europe. France, with 2½ to 3 milliards (francs) 5½ to 6 hundred million dollars in the bank and among the public, would feel grateful to you were the unlimited free coinage bill to become a law. You would get from France alone $300,000,000, and that quickly. I know that when silver was quoted at 54½ a short time ago, in London, high-placed officials in the bank favored sending a part of the bank's silver to you. Germany has an immense stock of silver bars which you would get; so have Italy and several other countries in Europe. India would send you immense amounts of silver instead of sending the same to China. England would be greatly benefited by unlimited free coinage with you. London, with a gold standard, would become more than ever the centre of the world's banking business. I cannot, and no sane man in Europe can, believe that the Congress of the United States will vote such a bill, with its unavoidable disastrous consequences."

But it is argued,—and this is the stock argument of Mr. St. John of New York,— France wouldn't send over her silver because, forsooth, she coins at a valuation of $1.33 an ounce, whereas we coin at a valuation of $1.29. They reason that she would lose 4 per cent. plus the cost of transportation and insurance by the operation. Unquestionably, no individual citizen of France would send over French silver coin to exchange below its home value. But how about the bank of France? Let us exert our imagination:

Time: Early in 1892. Place: Paris. Scene:

Directors' room of the Bank of France. A meeting of the directors in session.

(I transpose all sums mentioned in dollars.)

Director—How much silver have we in our vaults?

Chairman—About $250,000,000.

Director—What did that cost us?

Chairman—About $1.33 an ounce.

Director—What is silver worth now?

Chairman—About ninety-five cents an ounce.

Director—What loss does that represent?

Chairman—About $95,000,000.

All the Directors drum on the table nervously and inspect the flies on the ceiling. Suddenly a messenger enters and, in breathless haste, informs the board that an island has been discovered in the Pacific, the inhabitants of which are willing to exchange five million ounces of gold for silver at the rate of $1.29 an ounce. The information is secret and unquestionably reliable. The excitement is great. One of the Directors whips out a pencil and makes the following calculation: Five million ounces of gold is worth about 103 millions of dollars. With silver at $1.29 an ounce, the islanders will exchange that for eighty million ounces of silver. The five million ounces of gold will then at present price buy 110 million ounces of silver. Profit to the Bank of France, thirty million ounces of silver. Would they do it? Let Mr. St. John reply.

In this connection I wish briefly to point out two fallacies. One point often made is: "If silver rises in value here, it will rise in

Europe also. Why then should they send it here?" The fact that holders of European silver might ask even $1.29 for the silver ounce would not prove that they could find buyers in Europe who would pay $1.29. Certainly, no one would buy it at that price unless necessity compelled him to buy. But here in the United States, under free coinage, the law WOULD COMPEL US TO BUY SILVER AT $1.29 AN OUNCE. If I owe you a debt, the law will compel you to buy my silver at $1.29 an ounce in payment of that debt. If I go into your store and purchase anything, the law will compel you to buy my silver at $1.29 an ounce with your goods. Free silver coinage will make us forced buyers of silver at an exaggerated value.

The other fallacy is: "How will gold go out? It only goes in the balance of exchange." Under normal conditions, that is true. But the moment gold goes to a premium, gold becomes a merchandise, and unless silver rises to and remains permanently at $1.29, gold would be the most profitable merchandise to export.

DISTURBANCE TO BUSINESS.

The shock to business would be frightful. Take one item: The savings banks of the

United States have estimated deposits of over $1,600,000,000. Most of these banks limit deposit accounts to $1,000. This money represents the savings of mechanics, of poor women, and of the laboring class generally. Their loans, principally real estate mortgages, amount to $980,000,000. If we hear of the failure of a savings bank with a loss of a million, we justly think it a calamity.

Free silver coinage, even if the value of the silver dollar advanced permanently from 73 to 80 cents (which I most vehemently dispute), would represent a loss to these stockholders of 20 per cent.—equivalent to the failure and total collapse of nearly 200 of these banks for a million dollars each. Try to conceive such an upheaval!

The principal merchants of St Louis, some 150, representing a relation to the business of the country of over $200,000,000, sent a memorial to Congress in February last, in which they said:

"We believe that the passage of the Senate bill, whilst the present unstable market values of silver obtain, would disturb the standard of values upon which all transactions, domestic and foreign, are based, would discourage for an indefinite period commercial intercourse, and depress the industries of the country in their varied directions. To agriculture, commerce and manufactures alike, we believe it would be prolific of the most serious results.

"We disclaim any antagonism to the use of silver in the currency of the country under conditions where its value in law will be honestly representative of its intrinsic or bullion value; but the experience of the past has demonstrated the futility of attempting to give a value to silver by special legislation which it does not intrinsically possess in the markets of the world."

Hon. Abram S. Hewitt, a citizen of whom New York is proud, one of the ablest men of our day—largely interested in silver mines and in the smelting of silver, wrote to the House committee in February:

"The greatest evil that can befall a nation is a change in the standard of value. Plagues, pestilence and famine are after all but local and temporary calamities; floods, earthquakes and cyclones are limited in their disastrous results, but a change in the standard of value affects all existing contracts, upsets all the calculations of business, reaches every family in the land and converts legitimate trade into speculation and gambling."

WHO SHALL LEAD US?

Under what leadership are we asked to take this momentous step? Until the American people learn to place faith in scientific and trained intelligence, they will stumble on from error to error. This silver question is distinctly a question of finance. The judgment of what class ought to be accepted as final in this question? If you wanted to have a question in astronomy answered to whom would you go? Not to the manufacturers of telescopes, nor to the men who polish the brass of the lenses. You would go to an astronomer, to a man who had made the study of the heavens his life work. If you want information as to a point of law you do not go to the publishers of law books, nor to the men who set the type or run the presses, but to the man who has devoted years to a study of the subject, to an attorney-at-law. So with reference to this question of money. The men whose advice sensible men should follow would be: Firstly, the authors on finance, the professors of political economy in our colleges, the men whose lives have been devoted to the study of questions relating to the monetary science. Secondly, the men who have practically handled money in large masses—men who have been financial officers of the United States—secretaries of the treasury, comptrollers of the currency, directors of the mint. Thirdly, the bankers of the country. To these classes, and not to silver miners or silver smelters or crafty politicians should a question like free silver coinage be submitted. And I defy the silver men to find one single financial author of distinction, one man who has ever been secretary of the treasury, comptroller of the currency, director of the mint, and, of the thousands of bankers, twenty representative men who will say that the free and unlimited coinage of silver is a safe measure.

But says the silver man, with a sneer, "The bankers are after their own interests." Who are the bankers and what is their interest? When the stockholders of a bank meet, whom do they select as directors? Their self-interest leads them to select men whose financial standing, known integrity and general character will command the respect of the business community. Whom do these directors elect as president and cashier? Again, the men who best represent the same characteristics. What is the interest of a banker? The banker's interest lies in the prosperity of his depositors and that again in the prosperity of the community. If the customers of a bank make money, the bank makes money. If their business is unsatisfactory, the business of the bank is necessarily in sympathy.

THE AGITATION SHOULD CEASE.

Whatever settlement is effected by this Congress as to silver, THE SILVER AGITATION SHOULD CEASE. The business interests of the country demand a rest. A year and a half ago, business was flourishing. Land found a ready sale. Labor was in great demand. In June, 1890, a test vote of the House of Representatives of 116 to 140, showed the country that by a change of only thirteen votes, both branches of Congress would endorse free silver coinage. Whether that was the cause or not, the fact cannot be disputed that from about that time business confidence has been lacking, capital has been timid, new enterprises have languished, and Colorado, with the whole country, has suffered. Silver men say the trouble began with the failure of the Barings. It certainly antedated that by several months. That failure intensified the strain exceedingly. Yet why have we not long ago recovered from its effects? The Barings' failure was the greatest possible advertisement as to the safety and security of our American stocks and bonds. That fact, with the uncertainty hanging over the political embroilments of Europe, should have operated to send European money here in a flood. What has kept it away? The fear of silver values. With a crop bountiful beyond compare, coincident with crop failures in Europe,—we should to-day be in the acme of prosperity. Yet 1891 has been a dull year. Everybody felt the pressure. Business was unsatisfactory. Land was not in demand. The demand for labor had diminished. In 1891, out of the forty-seven largest cities in the country, thirty-two cities increased their bank exchanges over 1890. Our young giant, Denver, was one of the fifteen cities which decreased. Denver exchanges: 1890—250 millions. 1891—228 millions,—a decrease of nearly 9 per cent. That tells volumes. Is it not time that our Colorado leaders for free silver, however earnest, however sincere, however loyal to Colorado, should realize that their agitation is holding back the prosperity and development of the State? Has not the hour come when men who realize the facts should speak out boldly and distinctly on this subject?

FOUR ALTERNATIVES.

I conclude with the following alternatives:

1. If you want to be conservative and unwilling to bring disaster to silver, you will want any legislation on the subject to be coupled with the declaration, that silver

coinage shall stop when gold goes to a premium. You will want the present law to stand for another presidential term while vigorous efforts shall be made to bring about international bimetallism. That, in order to bring about European co-operation, it will be necessary to recoin our silver at a ratio of 15½ : 1 seems to me too self-evident to need any argument.

2. If these efforts fail and if you are laboring for the CAUSE OF SILVER, that is if you are willing to make a temporary sacrifice in order to give it a permanently increased market value, then you should want all Government purchases of silver to stop, should want to sell silver abroad and pull in all the gold possible. Such action, to use Bismarck's simile, would make the gold blanket so short that some of the European nations would have their financial nakedness exposed. Then would come a repentant desire to accept an additional monetary silver blanket.

3. If you want silver to bring you $1.29 an ounce and that quickly, the only legislation is limited free coinage or coinage restricted to the American product. That will give the silver mine owner $1.29 instead of ninety-five cents for every ounce of silver—so long as gold is not advanced to a premium. It will give a tremendous boost to the

silver States. It will be a great Protective annual scoop of nearly twenty millions out of the pockets of the American people. So long as they can stand it, Colorado can. There will, however, come a day of reckoning—how soon or how long delayed, no man can tell.

4. If you want to pay a debt with a liberal discount and expect to die soon thereafter so as to escape the other disagreeable incidents of general business collapse, then you want free and unlimited silver coinage. If you want the value of silver to go up for a few points and then gradually to fall back to a value even below the ounce price of to-day, then by all means, you want the free and unlimited coinage of silver. Under such a policy, the words of "Ecclesiastes" will be speedily verified: "HE THAT LOVETH SILVER SHALL NOT BE SATISFIED WITH SILVER."

Louis R. Ehrich.

SUPPLEMENTARY NOTE.

Since the preceding pages were prepared for the press, I have been afforded an opportunity, through the courtesy of the Commonwealth Club of New York, of presenting in that city the conclusions at which I had arrived on the question of silver. A summary of these conclusions is given in the following recommendations :

The silver legislation which our financial condition demands is :

First.—A declaration that, if gold should rise to a premium, all government silver purchases should immediately cease. Such a declaration would operate powerfully against the possibility of a gold panic.

Second.—The present silver purchases should be reduced in some gradual proportion which would contemplate the cessation of all purchases within a period of say five years.

Third.—Such gradual reduction could, in a measure, be counterbalanced by an increase in our silver subsidiary currency. This at present is about $1.20 per capita. It could safely be increased to $3.00 per capita, which would mean a demand for about seventy-five million ounces of silver.

Fourth.—Free and unlimited trade with silver-using countries. Their taking our silver might even satisfy the plea of "reciprocity."

Fifth.—A call for an early "International Conference," a conference in which the most earnest efforts would be put forth to bring about a world agreement in behalf of genuine Bimetallism—a Bimetallism which would lift silver from its present discredited position, would link it firmly with gold as a world medium of exchange, and would establish a ratio so fixed and so permanent that all over the globe, for a long period of time, whether as bullion or as money, silver, as related to gold, would have one uniform, unchangeable value.

L. R. E.

February 24, 1892.

INDEX.

Act of 1834, p. 10; of 1873, p. 11; of 1890, p. 24.
Airy, Sir G. B., experience in France, in 1826, p. 65.
Agricultural Products, exports of, in 1891, p. 94.
Allison's Amendment, of 1878, p. 22.
Assignats, in France, p. 63.

Bankers, true interest of, p. 104.
Barings, effects of failure of, p.105.
Belford, Judge, statement in May, 1891, p. 74.
Benton, Thomas H., speech of, 1834, p. 72.
Bimetallism and Monometallism, p. 38.
Bland, first bill of, 1878, p. 22.
Bounties of the Silver-mine Owners, p. 37.
Boutwell, Geo. S., drafts bill of 1873, p. 18.
Business in the West, in 1891, p. 106; disturbance to, through free coinage, p. 100.

Cernuschi, testimony of, in Washington, 1876, pp. 51, 68, 69, 83, 96.
Chevalier, Michel, statement concerning ratio, p. 64.
Coinage of Silver, between 1873 and 1878, p. 47; suspended in Europe, p. 26.
Coinage Ratio, p. 20.
Coinage Regulated by the Constitution, p. 6.
Coinage act of 1792, p. 13; of 1853, p,. 13-14.
Colorado's interest in Silver Bounties, p. 37.
Colorado's interests opposed to Free Silver, p. 41.
Colorado's Development, hampered by silver agitation, p.41.
"Conspiracy" against silver of 1873, pp, 17-46.
Creditors, the real, p. 30.

Debtor Classes, the true, p. 30.
Debtors, expectations of, p. 25.
Debts in the West, payable in gold, p. 33.
Denver, decrease of business in, in 1891, p. 106.

Doctors disagree as to the dose, p. 46.
Demonetization of Silver, p. 17.
"Dollar of the Daddies," called for in 1834, p. 11.
Double Standard, 1853-1862, p. 15.
Dunham, D. C. L., statement of, 1853, p. 34.

Ehrich, Louis R., business interest in the rise of silver, p. 44.
England, drafts on France and the United States in 1892, p. 74.
England, silver coinage of, in 1891, p. 67.
Elliott, opinion of, 1873, p. 18.

Farmer, the, and his oxen, pp. 58-59.
Farmers, interests of, pp. 29-93.
Farmer, American, basis on which his sales are made, p. 35; a creditor as well as a debtor, p. 94.
Farmer, receipts of, for his products, how regulated, p. 95.
Farm Mortgages of the West, p. 30.
Feer-Herzog, statement in 1878, pp. 90-97; death in 1881, p. 52.
France, Bank of, directors' meeting, (as imagined) in 1892, p. 99; stock of silver in, p. 97.
France, recent financial history of, pp. 61, 62, 63.
France, quoted by Thomas as bimetallic, p. 61.
Forssell, opinion on the practicability of bimetallism by a single State, p. 85.
Free Coinage, if authorized, should be limited to the American product, p. 36; results of, p. 27.

Germany demonetizes Silver, 1873, p. 66; adopts gold standard, 1871-1873, p. 17.
Gold, production of 1841-1851, p. 12; production after 1850, p. 16.
Gold and silver, relative production of, 1841-1850, p. 54.
Gold, increased production of 1848, 1849 and 1852, p. 65.
Gold as merchandise, p. 100.
Gold, discoveries of 1849-1851, p. 12.
Gold coinage in 1814, p. 9; of the United States, p. 27.
Gold disappearance and Silver inundation, p. 96.
Gold product in 1890, p. 21.
Gorham's speech in 1834, p. 12.
Gresham's Law, p. 8.

Hamilton, Alexander, report for establishment of mint, p. 6; recommends ratio of gold to silver as 1 to 15, p. 7.
Hayes, President, vetoes bill of 1878, p. 22.
Hewitt, Abram S., statement to committee in 1891, p. 102; speech of 1876, on the charge of "Conspiracy," p. 47.

Hooper of Massachusetts introduces bill of 1873, p. 49.
Horton, Dana, authority as a bimetallist, p. 52; comments on the death of Ernest Seyd p. 53.

Imports and exports of United States, pp. 95–96.
Ingalls, speech of 1891, p. 19.
India, influences on prosperity of, by shifting prices of silver, p. 94. financial relations with England, p. 77.
India's absorption of Silver and Gold, 1851–1860, pp. 55–57.
Indian Cotton, p. 57.
Indian Breadstuffs, p. 57.
Interest, the rate of, for mortgages, p. 30.

Jackson, Andrew, currency message of, p. 32.
Jevons, the reservoir simile of, pp. 80–81.
Jones, Senator, prediction of, p. 89.
Jones and Bogy, Senators, report of, 1876, p. 51.

Kelley, W. L. opinion of, 1873, p. 19.
Knox, John Jay, before committee on coinage, 1891, p. 18.

Latin Monetary Union, organized in 1865, p. 66; stops free coinage, p. 21.
Limits coinage of silver in 1874, p. 67; stops **coinage of** silver in 1878, p. 67.
Legal Tender act of 1862, p. 15.

Magnin, opinion of, p. 84.
Mallet, Sir Louis, on the possible policy of India, p. 91; on the shifting price of silver, p. 94.
Mandats in France, pp. 63–64.
Mining Congress at Denver, 1891, bimetallism resolution, pp. 38–39.
Mexico, results of free coinage in, p. 33.
Mexico and Bimetallism, p. 79.
Mexico, silver production of, p. 26.
Mint proposed by Jefferson and Morris, p. 6.
Mine-owners, expectations of, p. 25.
Monetary Conference at Paris in 1867, pp. 66–90; of 1881, p. 84.
Money, what constitutes, p. 69.
Money, value of in New York, November, 1891, p. 76.
Money, intrinsic value of, p. 72.
Money, per capita circulation in France, England, Germany, p. 73, in the United States, 1865–1891, p. 75.

Newcomb, Prof. Simon, statement of, 1879.
Nickel-miners, their claim for free coinage, p. 71.

Paris, International Conference at, 1881, p. 52.
Patterson's Opinion, p. 18.
Parieu, statement of, in 1886, p. 90.
Pierson, opinion of, on Gresham's law, p. 85.
Pirmez, M., statement in 1881, p. 97.
Price, fluctuations of 1890-1891, p. 24.

Resumption of Specie Payments in 1877-1879, p. 10.
Ruggles, answer of, to Prince Napoleon, p. 66.

St. John, opinion of, in 1891, p. 98.
St. Louis Merchants, memorial of, February 1891, p. 101.
Savings Banks, deposits in, p. 101.
Savings Bank depositors, losses to through free coinage, p. 101.
Seligman, William, letter of, December 1890, p. 97.
Senate, United States, said by Senator Ingalls to have been hypnotized in 1873, p. 50.
Seyd, Ernest, opinion of, p. 49; defense of the memory of, p. 50.
"Shortage" of Silver in 1876, p. 48.
Silver agitation should cease, p. 105.
Silver coinage bills of 1876-1877, p. 22;
Silver dollar demonetized in 1873, p. 17; disappears after 1840, p. 12.
Silver, fluctuations in the value of 1793-1892, pp. 86, 87, 88, 89.
Silver, forcing the buying of, p. 100; decrease in demand for, p. 56.
Silver production, large increase in, p. 27.
Silver, market value of, 1891-1692, p. 25; recent predictions concerning its advance in price, p. 85-86; price of, high water mark in 1859, p. 56; the world's stock of, p. 97; total production of, in United States, 1865-1891, p. 93; exports of, 1865-1891, p. 93; relative value of reduced by the hand of nature, p. 21; would free coinage cause a rise of its price in Europe? p. 100.
Snowden's Opinion, p. 18.
Stewart, Senator, of Nevada, pp. 20-89.
Stoughton, opinion of, 1873, p. 19.
Sumter, first shot at, p 15.
Supply and demand regulate value of money metals, pp. 53-54.
Symes, opinion of, on bimetallism, p. 86.

Teller, Senator, speech in January, 1892, p. 89.
Ten miners, the, p. 91.
Thomas, Charles S., paper on the silver question, p. 42.
Trans-mississippi Congress of 1891, bimetallism resolution, pp. 38-39.
Vest, Senator, speech of January, 1892, p. 41.

Walker, F. A., statement before Congressional Committee, January, 1891, p. 82.
Webster, Daniel, opinion on circulating medium in 1815, p. 36.
Western opinions on Silver, p. 29.
White, Campbell P., statement of, 1831, p. 9.
Windom, Secretary, submits plan for silver coinage, 1890, p. 23.
Wolowski, opposition of, to gold standard, p. 53.

PENDING ISSUES.

Economic and Political Science.

Atkinson. **The Distribution of Products; or, the Mechanism and the Metaphysics of Exchange.** Three Essays. What Makes the Rate of Wages? What is a Bank? The Railway, the Farmer, and the Public. By EDWARD ATKINSON. Second edition, revised and enlarged, with new statistical material. 8vo, cloth . . $1 50

"It would be difficult to mention another book that gives so effective a presentation of the present conditions and methods of industry, and of the marvels that have been wrought in the arts of production and transportation during the past fifty years."—*Advertiser*, Boston.

Cossa. **Taxation, Its Principles and Methods.** A Translation of the "First Principles of the Science of Finance." By Professor LUIGI COSSA, Ph.D., of the University of Pavia. Edited with notes by HORACE WHITE 1 00

Moore. **Friendly Sermons to Protectionists and Manufacturers.** By J. S. MOORE. (Economic Monograph, No. 4) . . 25

O'Neil. **The American Electoral System.** An Analysis of Its Character and Its History. By CHARLES A. O'NEIL, of the New York Bar. 12mo, ... 1 50

"The author's plans and compilations will be found valuable, and the book is well worth having and studying."—*Ohio State Journal*.

"We hail as hopeful the appearance of any thoughtful work on this vital subject, Mr. O'Neil has given us a timely and valuable book."—*Public Opinion*, Washington.

"Mr. O'Neil's book is full of valuable suggestions, and deserves a careful reading by all who are interested in our political system."—*Boston Traveller*.

Schoenhof. **The Industrial Situation and the Question of Wages.** A Study in Social Physiology. By J. SCHOENHOF, author of "The Destructive Influence of the Tariff," etc. (Questions of the Day Series, No. XXX.) 8vo, cloth 1 00

—— **The Destructive Influence of the Tariff upon Manufacture and Commerce, and the Facts and Figures Relating Thereto.** By J. SCHOENHOF. (Questions of the Day Series, No. IX.) 8vo, cloth, 75 cents ; paper 40

"An able presentation of the subject by a practical man, which should have a wide circulation."

G. P. PUTNAM'S SONS, NEW YORK AND LONDON

Sumner. **Lectures on the History of Protection in the United States.** By Prof. W. G. SUMNER, of Yale College. 8vo, cloth extra 75

"There is nothing in the literature of free trade more forcible and effective than this little book."—*N. Y. Evening Post.*

Sterne. **The Constitutional History and Political Development of the United States.** An Analytical Study. By SIMON STERNE, of the New York Bar. Second edition, revised with editions. 12mo, cloth 1 25

Taussig. **The Tariff History of the United States, 1789-1888.** Comprising the material contained in "Protection to Young Industries" and "History of the Present Tariff," together with the revisions and additions needed to complete the narrative. By Prof. F. W. TAUSSIG. 12mo, cloth. (Questions of the Day Series, No. XLVII.) 1 25

"Tracts like this will be read by many who would not open a bulky volume of the same title, and they will find that what they regarded as the most confused and perplexing of subjects is not only comprehensible, but also interesting."—*The Nation.*

The President's Message. With Annotations of Facts and Figures. By R. R. BOWKER. (Questions of the Day Series, No. XLIX.) 25

A republication, in convenient form for reference, of the clear and business-like statement made by President Cleveland, in his latest message to Congress, of the economical issues now before the country for decision.

Wells. **Practical Economics.** A collection of Essays respecting certain of the Economic Experiences of the United States. By DAVID A. WELLS. 8vo, cloth 1 50

CHIEF CONTENTS.—A Modern Financial Utopia—The True Story of the Leaden Images—The Taxation of Distilled Spirits—Recent Phases of the Tariff Question—Tariff Revision—The Pauper-Labor Argument—The Silver Question—Measures of Value—The Production and Distribution of Wealth.

—————— **Our Merchant Marine.** How it Rose, Increased, became Great, Declined and Decayed. By DAVID A. WELLS. (Questions of the Day Series, No. III.)

—————— **Why We Trade and How We Trade,** or an enquiry into the extent to which the existing commercial and fiscal policy of the United States restricts the material prosperity and development of the country. By DAVID A. WELLS. (Economic Monograph, No. 1) . 25

www.ingramcontent.com/pod-product-compliance
Lightning Source LLC
Chambersburg PA
CBHW020135170426
43199CB00010B/750